MVFOL

Discovering & Exploring

HABITS OF MIND

Edited by
ARTHUR L. COSTA
and
BENA KALLICK

Association for Supervision and Curriculum Development
Alexandria, Virginia USA

Association for Supervision and Curriculum Development
1703 N. Beauregard St. • Alexandria, VA 22311-1714 USA
Telephone: 1-800-933-2723 or 703-578-9600 • Fax: 703-575-5400
Web site: http://www.ascd.org • E-mail: member@ascd.org

Gene R. Carter, *Executive Director*
Michelle Terry, *Associate Executive Director, Program Development*
Nancy Modrak, *Director, Publishing*
John O'Neil, *Director of Acquisitions*
Julie Houtz, *Managing Editor of Books*
Margaret Oosterman, *Associate Editor*
René Bahrenfuss, *Copy Editor*
Charles D. Halverson, *Project Assistant*
Gary Bloom, *Director, Design and Production Services*
Georgia McDonald, *Senior Designer*
Tracey A. Smith, *Production Manager*
Dina Murray, *Production Coordinator*
John Franklin, *Production Coordinator*
M. L. Coughlin Editorial Services, *Indexer*

ASCD publications present a variety of viewpoints. The views expressed or implied in this book should not be interpreted as official positions of the Association.

Printed in the United States of America.

February 2000 member book (p). ASCD Premium, Comprehensive, and Regular members periodically receive ASCD books as part of their membership benefits. No. FY00-5.

ASCD Stock No. 100032
ASCD member price: $16.95   nonmember price: $20.95

Library of Congress Cataloging-in-Publication Data
Discovering and exploring habits of mind / edited by Arthur L. Costa
and Bena Kallick.
         p. cm. — (Habits of mind ; bk. 1)
Includes bibliographical references and index.
"ASCD stock no. 100032"—T.p. verso.
     ISBN 0-87120-368-5 (alk. paper)
   1. Thought and thinking—Study and teaching—United States. 2.
Cognition in children—United States. 3. Intellect. I. Costa, Arthur
L. II. Kallick, Bena. III. Series.
     LB1590.3 .D6 2000
     155.4'13—dc21
                         99-050943

04 03 02 01 00   10 9 8 7 6 5 4 3 2 1

Native peoples teach that the ultimate norm for morality is the impact our choices have on persons living seven generations from now. If the results appear good for them, then our choices are moral ones; if not, they are immoral.

We therefore dedicate Habits of Mind: A Developmental Series to our children, our grandchildren, and their children's children.

HABITS OF MIND: A DEVELOPMENTAL SERIES

DISCOVERING AND EXPLORING HABITS OF MIND

SERIES FOREWORD: THINKING ON THE ROAD OF LIFE

DAVID PERKINS

While driving into town a few years ago, I found myself behind a young man in a red convertible. Like many people, I have certain expectations about young men in red convertibles, but this young man surprised me. When we reached a railroad crossing, he was painfully careful. He slowed down as he approached the tracks. The closer he got to the tracks, the more he slowed. As his car passed over the tracks, it hardly was moving at all. At this point, with great care, the young man looked to the left, and then he looked to the right. No train was coming. Satisfied with his safety, he gunned the engine and sped off. The young man was careful—and yet he wasn't! Surely, the middle of the tracks isn't the best position from which to scan for oncoming trains!

This man's behavior provides a kind of a metaphor for the mission of the four-book series Habits of Mind: A Developmental Series. When on the road of life, we ought to be thoughtful about what we are doing. For example, we ought to manage impulsivity and strive for accuracy, two of the worthwhile habits of mind this series describes. Yet if good thinking is to help us out in life, it has to go on the road with us. The trouble is, good thinking often gets left behind altogether, or it's exercised in flawed ways that don't do the job, as this young man demonstrated.

How can we encourage ourselves and others—particularly students—to take good thinking on the road? Habits of Mind: A Developmental Series explores one answer to that challenge: the cultivation of habits of mind, or habits of thought as John Dewey (1933) called them. The idea is that we should have habits of mind such as persistence and flexible thinking, just as we have habits like brushing our teeth or putting the dog out or being kind to people. Habits are not behaviors we pick up and lay down whimsically or arbitrarily. They are behaviors we exhibit reliably on appropriate occasions, and they are smoothly triggered without painstaking attention.

The very notion of habits of mind, however, poses a conceptual puzzle. By definition, habits are routine, but good use of the mind is not. The phrase habits of mind makes for a kind of oxymoron, like "loud silence" or "safe risk." Indeed, the story of the young man in the convertible illustrates what can go wrong with cultivating habits of mind. Here you have a habit of mind (being careful) played out in a way that misses the point (the man looks for the train from the middle of the tracks!). The very automaticity of a habit can undermine its function. Habits like that don't serve us well on a literal highway—or on the metaphorical road of life, either.

Can one have a habit of mind that truly does its work? The resolution to this puzzle is not very difficult. There's a difference between the thinking required to manage a mental process and the thinking done by the process. A habitual mental process does not require a lot of management to launch and sustain it, but that process itself may conduct mindful thinking. It may involve careful examination of alternatives, assessment of risks and consequences, alertness to error, and so on. For example, I have a simple, well-entrenched habit for the road of life: looking carefully when I depart a setting to be sure that I'm not leaving anything behind. This habit triggers and runs off reliably, with very little need for mindful management. But the behaviors deployed by the habit are highly mindful: scrutinizing the setting, glancing under chairs for concealed objects, and peering into drawers and closets for overlooked items.

In all fairness, the man in the convertible displayed a habit with something of this quality, too. It was good that he looked both ways with care. No doubt his scan of the tracks was precise and sensitive. He certainly would have detected any oncoming train. The difficulty was that his habit included a bug, rather like a bug in a computer program. Although his habit had a thoughtful phase (scanning the tracks), he was not thoughtful about his habit (choosing the point where he should scan the tracks).

Thus, the idea of habits of mind is not self-contradictory. A behavior can be habitual in its management but mindful in what it does. Still, one might ask, "Why not have it all? Ideally, shouldn't thinking processes be mindfully managed, mindful through and through for that extra edge?" Probably not! At least three things are wrong with this intuitively appealing ideal.

First, having to manage a thinking process mindfully would likely reduce the thoughtfulness of the process itself. As Herbert Simon (1957) and many other psychologists have emphasized, we humans have a limited capacity for processing information. Committing the management of a thinking process to routine is one way to open up mental space for the work the process has to do. Second, life has many distractions and preoccupations. A well-developed habit is more likely to make its presence felt than a practice that always must be deployed with meticulous deliberateness.

The third objection to this ideal of thoroughly mindful thinking goes beyond these pragmatic considerations to a logical point. Suppose the general rule is that thinking processes need mindful management. Surely managing a thinking process is itself a thinking process, so that process, too, needs mindful management. And the process of managing that needs mindful management, and so on. It is mindful management all the way up, an infinite tower of metacognition, each process managed by its own mindfully managed manager. Clearly this approach won't work. Enter habits of mind, an apt challenge to a misguided conception of thinking as thoroughly thoughtful.

The notion of habits of mind also challenges another conception: the notion of intelligence. Most of the research on human intelligence is emphatically "abilities centric" (Perkins, Jay, & Tishman, 1993; Perkins, 1995). As mentioned in Chapter 1 of Book 1, the IQ tradition sees intelligence as a pervasive, monolithic mental ability, summed up by IQ and Charles Spearman's (1904) "g" factor, a statistical construct representing general intelligence. A number of theorists have proposed that there are many kinds of mental ability (two to 150, according to one model developed by Guilford [1967]). Although this book is not a setting where these models bear review (see Perkins, 1995), most of these models have something in common: They treat intelligence as an "ability on demand." Intelligence becomes a matter of what you can do when you know what it is that you're supposed to try to do (such as complete this analogy, decide whether this inference is warranted, or find the best definition for this word).

Thinking in much of life is a different matter. In daily life, we not only have to solve problems, we also have to find them amid an ongoing, complex stream of stimuli imposing constant demands and distractions. On the road of life, our thinking is not just a matter of the thinking we can do when we know a peak performance is demanded. It also is a matter of our sensitivity to occasions and our inclination to invest ourselves in them thoughtfully. High mental ability alone may serve us well when we're sitting at a desk, our pencils poised, but good habits of mind keep us going in the rest of the world. This point is underscored by scholars such as philosopher Robert Ennis (1986), with his analysis of critical thinking dispositions; psychologist Jonathan Baron (1985), with his dispositional model of intelligence; and psychologist Ellen Langer (1989), with her conception of mindfulness.

A program of empirical research on thinking dispositions, which my colleague Shari Tishman and I have directed over the past several years, underscores what's at stake here (e.g., Perkins & Tishman, 1997). Working with students from middle to late elementary school, we investigated their performance on a variety of critical and creative thinking tasks involving narratives. Over and over again, we found that they could do far better than they did do when they explored options, considered pros and cons, and performed similar tasks. Their performance was limited because they often did not detect when such moves were called for. When they did detect what they should do, or when the places were pointed out, they easily could show the kind of thinking called for. They didn't lack intelligence in the sense of ability on demand, but they lacked the habits of mind that provide for ongoing alertness to shortfalls in thinking.

In that spirit, this series of four books speaks not just to intelligence in the laboratory but also to intelligent behavior in the real world. It addresses how we can help youngsters get ready for the road of life, a sort of "drivers' education" for the mind. Imagine what life would be like without good habits of various sorts. Our teeth would rot, our bodies collapse, our gardens wither, our tempers sour, and our friends drift away. We do better to the extent that we get direction from good habits, including habits of mind. When today's students hit the road, the ideas in Habits of Mind: A Developmental Series can help them ride on smooth mental wheels, checking for trains *before* they start over the tracks!

REFERENCES

Baron, J. (1985). *Rationality and intelligence.* New York: Cambridge University Press.

Dewey, J. (1933). *How we think: A restatement of the relation of reflective thinking to the education process.* New York: D. C. Heath.

Ennis, R. H. (1986). A taxonomy of critical thinking dispositions and abilities. In J. B. Baron & R. S. Sternberg (Eds.), *Teaching thinking skills: Theory and practice* (pp. 9–26). New York: W. H. Freeman.

Guilford, J. P. (1967). *The nature of human intelligence.* New York: McGraw-Hill.

Langer, E. J. (1989). *Mindfulness.* Reading, MA: Addison-Wesley.

Perkins, D. N. (1995). *Outsmarting IQ: The emerging science of learnable intelligence.* New York: The Free Press.

Perkins, D. N., Jay, E., & Tishman, S. (1993). Beyond abilities: A dispositional theory of thinking. *The Merrill-Palmer Quarterly, 39*(1), 1–21.

Perkins, D. N., & Tishman, S. (1997). *Dispositional aspects of intelligence.* Paper presented at the Second Spearman Seminar, The University of Plymouth, Devon, England.

Simon, H. A. (1957). *Models of man: Social and rational.* New York: Wiley.

Spearman, C. (1904). General intelligence, objectively defined and measured. *American Journal of Psychology, 15,* 201–209.

PREFACE TO THE SERIES

ARTHUR L. COSTA AND BENA KALLICK

Donna Norton Swindal, a resource teacher in Burnsville, Minnesota, recently shared an interesting story about a 4th grader who brought a newspaper clipping to class. The article described genocide in a troubled African country. After a lively discussion about what was happening there, one concerned classmate stated, "If those people would just learn to persist, they could solve their problems."

His philosophical colleague added, "If they would learn to listen with understanding and empathy, they wouldn't have this problem."

Yet another activist suggested, "We need to go over there and teach them the habits of mind!"

What are the "habits of mind" these concerned young citizens were so eager to share? They are the overarching theme of Habits of Mind: A Developmental Series, and they are the heart of the book you now hold in your hands.

THE BEGINNING

The ideas in Habits of Mind: A Developmental Series first started in 1982. Our beginning conversations about Intelligent Behaviors flourished into rich experiments with classroom practitioners until finally we arrived at this juncture: a series of four books to inspire the work of others. In our daily work with students and staff, we discovered that names were needed for the behaviors that would be expected from one another if, indeed, we were living in a productive learning organization. We came to call these dispositions "habits of mind," indicating that the behaviors require a discipline of the mind that is practiced so it becomes a habitual way of working toward more thoughtful, intelligent action.

The intent of Habits of Mind: A Developmental Series is to help educators teach toward these habits of mind, which we see as broad, enduring, and essential lifespan learnings that are as appropriate for adults as they are for students. Our hope is that by teaching students (and adults) the habits of mind, students will be more disposed to draw upon the habits when they are faced with uncertain or challenging situations. And, ultimately, we hope the habits will help educators develop thoughtful, compassionate, and cooperative human beings who can live productively in an increasingly chaotic, complex, and information-rich world (as the 4th graders above so aptly demonstrated!).

THE HABITS OF MIND

The following list contains the habits of mind described in Habits of Mind: A Developmental Series. The habits begin with the individual and move out to the entire community. Keep in mind, however, that the list is not complete. As our conversations continue—as you work with the habits, too—we all will likely identify other habits that should be added to this list.

The 16 habits of mind we have identified are

- Persisting
- Managing impulsivity
- Listening with understanding and empathy
- Thinking flexibly
- Thinking about thinking (metacognition)
- Striving for accuracy
- Questioning and posing problems
- Applying past knowledge to new situations
- Thinking and communicating with clarity and precision
- Gathering data through all senses
- Creating, imagining, innovating
- Responding with wonderment and awe
- Taking responsible risks
- Finding humor
- Thinking interdependently
- Remaining open to continuous learning

The most powerful communities use these habits of mind to guide all their work. Yet sometimes the practicality of school life requires that people make individual commitments with the hope that their beliefs and behaviors will affect the whole. Teaching with the habits of mind requires a shift toward a broader conception of educational outcomes and how they are cultivated, assessed, and communicated. Taken together, the four books in Habits of Mind: A Developmental Series aims to help you work toward and achieve these goals.

A DUAL PURPOSE

In this four-book series, we provide

- Descriptions and examples of the habits of mind.
- Instructional strategies intended to foster acquisition of these habits at school and at home.
- Assessment tools that provide a means of gathering evidence of student growth in the habits of mind.
- Ways of involving students, teachers, and parents in communicating progress toward acquiring the habits of mind.
- Descriptions from schools, teachers, and administrators about how they have incorporated the habits of mind and the effects of their work.

Our true intent for these books, however, is far more panoramic, pervasive, and long-range. Each book in the series works at two levels. The first level encompasses immediate and practical considerations that promote using the habits of mind in classrooms and schools every day. The second level addresses a larger, more elevated concern for creating a learning culture that considers habits of mind as central to building a thoughtful community. We summarize these levels as follows.

BOOK 1: DISCOVERING AND EXPLORING HABITS OF MIND

Level 1: Defining the habits of mind and understanding the significance of developing these habits as a part of lifelong learning.

Level 2: Encouraging schools and communities to elevate their level and broaden their scope of curricular outcomes by focusing on more essential, enduring lifespan learnings.

BOOK 2: *ACTIVATING AND ENGAGING HABITS OF MIND*

Level 1: Learning how to teach the habits directly and to reinforce them throughout the curriculum.

Level 2: Enhancing instructional decision making to employ content not as an end of instruction but as a vehicle for activating and engaging the mind.

BOOK 3: *ASSESSING AND REPORTING ON HABITS OF MIND*

Level 1: Learning about a range of techniques and strategies for gathering evidence of students' growth in and performance of the habits of mind.

Level 2: Using feedback to guide students to become self-assessing and to help school teams and parents use assessment data to cultivate a more thoughtful culture.

BOOK 4: *INTEGRATING AND SUSTAINING HABITS OF MIND*

Level 1: Learning strategies for extending the impact of habits of mind throughout the school community.

Level 2: Forging a common vision among all members of the educational community from kindergarten through post-graduate work: teachers, administrative teams, administrators, librarians, staff developers, teacher educators, school board members, and parents. This vision describes the characteristics of efficacious and creative thinkers and problem solvers.

In teaching for the habits of mind, we are interested in not only how many answers students know but also how students behave when they don't know an answer. We are interested in observing how students produce knowledge rather than how they merely reproduce it. A critical attribute of intelligent human beings is not only having information but also knowing how to act on it.

By definition, a problem is any stimulus, question, task, phenomenon, or discrepancy, the explanation for which is not immediately known. Intelligent behavior is performed in response to such questions and problems. Thus, we are interested in focusing on student performance under those challenging conditions—dichotomies, dilemmas, paradoxes, ambiguities and enigmas—that demand strategic reasoning, insightfulness, perseverance, creativity and craftsmanship to resolve them.

Teaching toward the habits of mind is a team effort. Because repeated opportunities over a long period are needed to acquire these habits of mind, the entire staff must dedicate itself to teaching toward, recognizing, reinforcing, discussing, reflecting on, and assessing the habits of mind. When students encounter these habits at each grade level in the elementary years and in each classroom throughout the secondary day—and when the habits also are reinforced and modeled at home—they become internalized, generalized, and habituated.

We need to find new ways of assessing and reporting growth in the habits of mind. We cannot measure process-oriented outcomes using old-fashioned, product-oriented assessment techniques. Gathering evidence of performance and growth in the habits of mind requires "kid watching." As students interact with real-life, day-to-day problems in school, at home, on the playground, alone, and with friends, teaching teams and other adults can collect anecdotes and examples of written and visual expressions that reveal students' increasingly voluntary and spontaneous use of these habits of mind. This work also takes time. The habits are never fully mastered, though they do become increasingly apparent over time and with repeated experiences and opportunities to practice and reflect on their performance.

Considered individually, each book helps you start down a path that will lead to enhanced curriculum, instruction, and assessment practices. Taken together, the books in the Habits of Mind: A Developmental Series provide a road map for individuals, for classrooms, and ultimately for a full-system approach. For our purposes, we think a "system" is approached when the habits of mind are integrated throughout the culture of the organization. That is, when all individual members of a learning community share a common vision of the attributes of effective and creative problem solvers, when resources are allocated to the development of those dispositions; when strategies to enhance those characteristics in themselves and others are planned, and when members of the organization join in efforts to continuously assess, refine, and integrate those behaviors in their own and the organization's practices.

> I can tell you right now that we will never be able to forget the habits of mind. They helped us so much! They taught us better ways of doing things and how to resolve problems! We learned respect and manners. My mother was so very impressed with this teaching. Also we learned that you need to get along with others and not to disrespect them either.
>
> Excerpted from a 5th grader's
> valedictorian address upon graduation from
> Friendship Valley Elementary School, Westminster, Maryland

PREFACE TO BOOK 1

ARTHUR L. COSTA AND BENA KALLICK

In the first book of this series, *Discovering and Exploring Habits of Mind*, the Habits of Mind are defined and described. Their place in the curriculum is also demonstrated. The chapters in this book include detailed explanations of 16 habits of mind, which are defined as dispositions displayed by intelligent people in response to problems, dilemmas, and enigmas, the resolutions of which are not immediately apparent.

THE HABITS OF MIND

Briefly, the habits of mind can be described as follows:

1. *Persisting.* Stick to it. See a task through to completion, and remain focused.

2. *Managing impulsivity.* Take your time. Think before you act. Remain calm, thoughtful, and deliberate.

3. *Listening with understanding and empathy.* Seek to understand others. Devote mental energy to another person's thoughts and ideas. Hold your own thoughts in abeyance so you can better perceive another person's point of view and emotions.

4. *Thinking flexibly.* Look at a situation another way. Find a way to change perspectives, generate alternatives, and consider options.

5. *Thinking about thinking (metacognition).* Know your knowing. Be aware of your own thoughts, strategies, feelings, and actions—and how they affect others.

6. *Striving for accuracy.* Check it again. Nurture a desire for exactness, fidelity, and craftsmanship.

7. *Questioning and posing problems.* How do you know? Develop a

questioning attitude, consider what data are needed, and choose strategies to produce those data. Find problems to solve.

8. *Applying past knowledge to new situations.* Use what you learn. Access prior knowledge, transferring that knowledge beyond the situation in which it was learned.

9. *Thinking and communicating with clarity and precision.* Be clear. Strive for accurate communication in both written and oral form. Avoid overgeneralizations, distortions, and deletions.

10. *Gathering data through all senses.* Use your natural pathways. Gather data through all the sensory paths: gustatory, olfactory, tactile, kinesthetic, auditory, and visual.

11. *Creating, imagining, innovating.* Try a different way. Generate novel ideas, and seek fluency and originality.

12. *Responding with wonderment and awe.* Let yourself be intrigued by the world's phenomena and beauty. Find what is awesome and mysterious in the world.

13. *Taking responsible risks.* Venture out. Live on the edge of your competence.

14. *Finding humor.* Laugh a little. Look for the whimsical, incongruous, and unexpected in life. Laugh at yourself when you can.

15. *Thinking interdependently.* Work together. Truly work with and learn from others in reciprocal situations.

16. *Remaining open to continuous learning.* Learn from experiences. Be proud—and humble enough—to admit you don't know. Resist complacency.

ORGANIZATION OF THE BOOK

Drawing on years of experience and research, noted author and educator David Perkins, in the foreword, focuses attention on the dispositions of a disciplined thinker and the use of habits of mind in everyday life. Chapter 1 examines the habits of mind in the context of intelligence. It develops a historical perspective on the changing conception of intelligence and traces how the understanding of intelligence has been transformed—from a static score produced on a test to a dynamic concept of modifiable capacities, which can be continuously developed throughout a person's lifetime and cultivated deliberately in homes, classrooms, and learning organizations. It also addresses their relationship to other educational trends, issues, and programs.

Chapter 2 defines 16 habits of mind and their relationship to enhancing intellectual capabilities. For each habit of mind an icon serves as a visual reminder of that particular habit and its meaning.

In Chapter 3, Shari Tishman, an eminently well-qualified writer and researcher in the area of thinking disputations, explains the benefits of focusing on habits of mind as educational outcomes and makes the case for their inclusion in curriculum and instruction.

Chapter 4 explores how the habits of mind fit into the overall curriculum and describes the relationship between learning activities, content, and thinking skills and processes.

In Chapter 5, Marian Leibowitz explores corporate mission statements, organizational rules, and workplace norms. She reminds us that when students enter the world of work, they will encounter expectations similar to those reflected in the habits of mind. She invites schools and classrooms to become laboratories to prepare students today for the demands of their future careers.

Drawing on experiences, testimonies, and research, Chapter 6 describes how the habits of mind affect teachers, students, and school staffs when they are adopted and infused throughout the school community.

Chapter 7 concludes with practical recommendations for moving to action. It suggests ways of acquainting staff members and students with the habits of mind, and it also proposes ways to inform and educate parents and the community about the habits of mind. As you consider this final chapter, you are invited to visualize how the habits of mind can become a shared vision for your school community.

CHANGING PERSPECTIVES ABOUT INTELLIGENCE

ARTHUR L. COSTA AND BENA KALLICK

What is intelligence if not the ability to face problems in an unpro-
grammed (creative) manner? The notion that such a nebulous socially
defined concept as intelligence might be identified as a "thing" with a
locus in the brain and a definite degree of heritability—and that it might
be measured as a single number thus permitting a unilinear ranking of
people according to the amount they possess[—]is a principal error. . . [,]
one that has reverberated throughout the country and has affected millions
of lives.

Stephen Jay Gould

The changing conception of intelligence is one of the most powerful, liberating forces ever to influence the restructuring of education, schools, and society. It also is a vital influence behind the development of the habits of mind, which are detailed more fully in the next chapter. To better understand those habits of mind, though, it is important to grasp how the concept of intelligence has changed over the last century. This chapter traces the evolution of conceptions of intelligence. It also considers how some of the significant researchers, educators, and psychologists influenced and transformed mental models of the intellect. This chapter goes on to show the relationship between the habits of mind and such other programs, theories, and trends in education as technology, multiple intelligences, and brain research.

INTELLIGENCE FOR A BYGONE ERA

At the turn of the 19th century in the United States, society was undergoing great shifts. Masses of immigrants poured into the nation, moving inland from their ports of entry or staying in the large eastern cities to fill the needs of the job-hungry Industrial Revolution. In retrospect, it is easy to see that the society of that day was elitist, racist, and sexist, its actions fueled by a fear of diluting "Anglo-Saxon purity." Employers of the time believed they needed a way to separate those who were educable and worthy of work from those who should be relegated to menial labor (or put back on the boat and shipped to their country of origin).

World War I contributed to homogenizing classes, races, and nationalities. Through military travels, enhanced communication, and industrialization, our population was becoming more cosmopolitan. A popular song of the time, "How Ya' Gonna Keep 'Em Down on the Farm After They've Seen Paree?" alerted the aristocracy to the impending trend toward globalization. Metaphorically the song proclaimed that to protect the existing separation of the masses into their "rightful" places, there was a need to analyze, categorize, separate, distinguish, and label human beings who were "not like us." Some means was necessary to measure individuals' and groups' "mental energies," to determine who was "fit" and who was not (Gould, 1981; Perkins, 1995).

Thanks to a mentality ruled by ideas of mechanism, efficiency, and authority, many came to believe that everything in life needed to be measured. Lord Kelvin, a 19th century physicist and astronomer, stated: "If you cannot measure it, if you cannot express it in numbers, your knowledge is of a very meager and unsatisfactory kind." Born in this era was Charles Spearman's theory of general intelligence. His theory was based on the idea that intelligence is inherited through genes and chromosomes and that it can be measured by one's ability to score sufficiently on Alfred Binet's Stanford-Binet Intelligence Test, yielding a static and relatively stable IQ score (Perkins, 1995, p. 42).

Immersed in the "efficiency" theories of the day, educators strived for the *one* best system for curriculum, learning, and teaching. Into this scene of educational management entered Edward L. Thorndike from Columbia University. He went beyond theory to produce usable educational tools including textbooks, tests, curriculums, and teacher training. Thorndike continues to wield a tremendous influence on educational practice. His "associationist" theory suggests that knowledge is a collection of links between pairs of external stimuli and internal mental responses. In this

2

context, learning is thought to be a matter of increasing the strength of the "good," or correct, bonds and decreasing the strength of the incorrect ones. Spearman's and Thorndike's theories still serve educators as a rationale for procedures such as tracking students according to high and low aptitude, the bell curve, drill and practice, competition, frequent testing, ability grouping, IQ scores as a basis for special education, task-analyzing learning into separate skills, and reinforcement of learning by rewards and external motivations (Resnick & Hall, 1998).

When people view their intelligence as a fixed and unchangeable entity, they strive to obtain positive evaluations of their ability and to avoid displaying evidence of inadequate ability. They believe their intelligence is demonstrated in task performance: They either have or lack ability. This negative self-concept influences effort. Effort and ability are negatively related in determining achievement, and having to expend great effort with a task is taken as a sign of low ability.

TOWARD A NEW VISION

Clearly, something new is needed if schools are to break out of this traditional, aptitude-centered mentality and make it possible for young people to acquire the kinds of mental habits needed to lead productive, fulfilling lives. We need a definition of intelligence that is as attentive to robust habits of mind as it is to the specifics of thinking processes or knowledge structures. We need to develop learning goals that reflect the belief that ability is a continuously expandable repertoire of skills, and that through a person's efforts, intelligence grows incrementally.

Incremental thinkers are likely to apply self-regulatory, metacognitive skills when they encounter task difficulties. They are likely to focus on analyzing the task and trying to generate and execute alternative strategies. They will try to garner internal and external resources for problem solving. When people think of their intelligence as something that grows incrementally, they are more likely to invest the energy to learn something new or to increase their understanding and mastery of tasks. They display continued high levels of task-related effort in response to difficulty. Learning goals are associated with the inference that effort and ability are positively related, so that greater efforts create and make evident more ability.

Children develop cognitive strategies and effort-based beliefs about their intelligence—the habits of mind associated with higher-order learning—when they continually are pressed to raise questions, accept challenges, find solutions that are not immediately apparent, explain concepts, justify their reasoning, and seek information. When we hold children accountable for this kind of intelligent behavior, they take it as a signal that we think they are smart, and they come to accept this judgment. The paradox is that children become smart by being treated as if they already are intelligent (Resnick & Hall, 1998).

A body of research deals with factors that seem to shape these habits, factors that have to do with people's beliefs about the relation between effort and ability. The following discussion traces the historical pathways of influential theories that have led to this new vision of intelligent behavior (Fogarty, 1997).

INTELLIGENCE CAN BE TAUGHT

Ahead of his time, Arthur Whimbey (Whimbey, Whimbey, & Shaw, 1975) urged us to reconsider our basic concepts of intelligence and to question the assumption that genetically inherited capacities are immutable. Whimbey argued that intelligence could be taught, and he provided evidence that certain interventions enhance the cognitive functioning of students from preschool to college level. Through instruction in problem solving, metacognition, and strategic thinking, Whimbey's students not only increased their IQ scores but also displayed more effective approaches to their academic work.

Participants in such studies, however, ceased using the cognitive techniques as soon as the specific conditions of training were removed. They became capable of performing the skill that was taught, but they acquired no general *habit* of using it and no capacity to judge for themselves when it was useful (Resnick & Hall, 1998).

To accommodate new learning, the brain builds more synaptic connections between and among its cells. It has been found that IQ scores have increased over the years (Kotulak, 1997). These increases demonstrate that instead of being fixed and immutable, intelligence is flexible and subject to great changes, both up and down, depending on the kinds of stimulation the brain gets from its environment.

STRUCTURE OF THE INTELLECT

J. P. Guilford and R. Hoeptner (1971) discerned 120 factors of the intellect. They believed that all students have intelligence, but they defined it as "what kind" instead of "how much." Guilford and his associates believed that intelligence consists of 120 thinking abilities that are combinations of operations, contents, and products. Operations include such mental capabilities as comprehending, remembering, and analyzing; contents refer to words, forms, and symbols; and products refer to complexity: single units, groups, and relationships.

Twenty-six of these factors were found relevant to school success. Tests were developed to profile students' abilities, and curriculum units and instructional strategies were developed to target, exercise, and enhance each of those 26 intellectual capacities. Guilford believed that through these interventions, a person's intelligence could be amplified.

THEORY OF COGNITIVE MODIFIABILITY

Iconoclast Reuven Feuerstein, working with disadvantaged children in Israel, challenges the prevailing notion of a fixed intelligence with his theory of cognitive modifiability. Feuerstein believes that intelligence is not a fixed entity but a function of experience and mediation by significant other individuals in a child's environment.

This modern theory underlies a fresh view of intelligence as modifiable: that intelligence can be taught, that human beings can continue to enhance their intellectual functioning throughout their lifetimes, and that all of us are "gifted" and all of us are "retarded" simultaneously (Feuerstein, Rand, Hoffman, & Miller, 1980).

MULTIPLE FORMS OF INTELLIGENCE

Howard Gardner (1983, 1999) believes that there are many ways of knowing, learning, and expressing knowledge. Gardner has identified several distinct intelligences that function in problem solving and in the creation of new products: verbal, logical/mathematical, kinesthetic, musical, spatial, naturalistic, interpersonal, and intrapersonal.

Gardner also believes that these intelligences can be nurtured in all human beings. Although each individual may have preferred forms, all of us can, with proper mediation and experience, continue to develop these capacities throughout our lifetime.

INTELLIGENCE AS SUCCESS IN LIFE

Robert Sternberg (1983) found that "mythological" IQ scores had little predictive quality in regard to success in later life. He argues for three types of intelligence:

• *Analytical intelligence* in which comparisons, evaluations, and assessments are made.
• *Creative intelligence* involving imagination, design, and invention.
• *Practical intelligence* in which use, practicality, and demonstration are paramount.

Sternberg believes that all human beings have the capacity to continue growing in these three domains, and he encourages educators to enhance them all (Sternberg, Torff, & Grigorenko, 1998).

LEARNABLE INTELLIGENCE

David Perkins (1995) further supports the theory that intelligence can be taught and learned. He believes that three important mechanisms underlie intelligence:

• *Neural intelligence* is the "genetically determined, hard-wired original equipment" that one has inherited and that determines the speed and efficiency of one's brain. Neural intelligence cannot be altered much.
• *Experiential intelligence* is context-specific knowledge that is accumulated through experience. It means knowing one's way around the various settings and contexts in which one functions. A person's reservoir of experiential intelligence can be expanded.
• *Reflective intelligence* is the "good use of the mind; the artful deployment of our faculties of thinking." It includes self-managing, self-monitoring, and self-modifying. Perkins refers to this capacity as "mindware" (Perkins, 1995, p. 264), and it can and should be cultivated.

EMOTIONAL INTELLIGENCE

Drawing on vast amounts of brain research, Daniel Goleman (1995) asserts that the intellect and emotions are inextricably intertwined. One cannot be developed without the other. Educating the emotions may be as important as educating the intellect. Helping people develop self-awareness, managing impulsivity and emotions, empathizing, and developing social skills are the most basic forms of intelligence. If these capacities are neglected, inadequacies may cause people to fall short of developing fuller intellectual capacities.

MORAL INTELLIGENCE

Robert Coles (1997) believes that children can become "more intelligent" by developing their inner character. He believes students develop a social/

moral intelligence by learning empathy, respect, reciprocity, cooperation, and how to live by the Golden Rule through the example of others and through explicit dialogue about moral issues. Coles believes that every child grows up by building a "moral archeology," a moral code of ethics through interactions with parents, peers, and significant others. He believes that this capacity can continue to be developed throughout a person's lifetime.

A FULLY DEVELOPED INTELLECT

Luis Alberto Machado (1980), former Venezuelan Minister of Intellectual Development, reminds us that all human beings have a basic right to the full development of their intellect. More and more government leaders in the United States and internationally are realizing that the level of a country's development depends on the level of intellectual development of its people. Industrial leaders realize that to survive and progress, any corporation must invest in its intellectual capital by continuing to enhance the mental resources of its employees. Educators, too, are realizing that our minds, bodies, and emotions must be engaged and transformed for learning to occur.

We must help students think powerfully about ideas, learn to critique as well as support others' thinking, and become thoughtful problem solvers and decision makers. The habits of mind provide a set of behaviors that discipline intellectual processes. They can be an integral component of instruction in every school subject, and they may determine achievement of any worthy goal as one moves out into life.

INTELLIGENT BEHAVIORS AS EDUCATIONAL OUTCOMES

Educational outcomes in traditional settings focus on how many answers a student knows. When we teach for the habits of mind, we also are interested in how students behave when they don't know an answer. The habits of mind are performed in response to questions and problems, the answers to which are not immediately known. We are interested in enhancing the ways students produce knowledge rather than how they merely reproduce it. We want students to learn how to develop a critical stance with their work: inquiring, editing, thinking flexibly, and learning from another person's perspective. The critical attribute of intelligent human beings is not only having information but also knowing how to act on it.

What behaviors indicate an efficient, effective thinker? What do human beings do when they behave intelligently? Research on effective thinking and intelligent behavior by Feuerstein and colleagues (1980), Glatthorn and Baron (1991), Sternberg (1984), Perkins (1991), Goleman (1995), and Ennis (1991) indicates that effective thinkers have identifiable characteristics. These characteristics have been identified in successful people in all walks of life: mechanics, teachers, entrepreneurs, salespeople, parents, scientists, artists, teachers, and mathematicians.

Horace Mann, a U.S. educator, once observed that, "Habit is a cable; we weave a thread of it each day, and at last we cannot break it" (1796–1859). In Habits of Mind: A Developmental Series, we focus on 16 habits of mind that teachers and parents can teach, cultivate, observe, and assess. The intent of these behaviors is to help students get into the habit of behaving intelligently. A habit of mind is a pattern of intellectual behaviors that leads to productive actions. When we experience dichotomies, are confused by dilemmas, or come face to face with uncertainties, our most effective response requires drawing forth certain patterns of intellectual behavior. When we draw upon these intellectual resources, the results are more powerful, of higher quality, and of greater significance than if we fail to employ such patterns of intellectual behavior.

A habit of mind is a composite of many skills, attitudes, cues, past experiences, and proclivities. It means that we value one pattern of intellectual behaviors over another; therefore, it implies making choices about which patterns should be used at a certain time. It includes a sensitivity to the contextual cues in a situation, which signal this circumstance as an appropriate time in which the application of this pattern would be useful. It requires a level of skillfulness to employ, carry out, and sustain the behaviors effectively. It suggests that as a result of each experience in which these behaviors were employed, the effects of their use are reflected upon, evaluated, modified, and carried forth to future applications. Figure 1.1 summarizes some of these attributes of the habits of mind.

While they are described in greater detail in Chapter 2, following is a list of 16 habits of mind:

1. Persisting
2. Managing impulsivity
3. Listening with understanding and empathy
4. Thinking flexibly
5. Thinking about thinking (metacognition)
6. Striving for accuracy

7. Questioning and posing problems
8. Applying past knowledge to new situations
9. Thinking and communicating with clarity and precision
10. Gathering data through all senses
11. Creating, imagining, innovating
12. Responding with wonderment and awe
13. Taking responsible risks
14. Finding humor
15. Thinking interdependently
16. Remaining open to continuous learning

FIGURE 1.1

Attributes of the Habits of Mind

The habits of mind attend to

Value: Choosing to employ a pattern of intellectual behaviors rather than other, less productive patterns.

Inclination: Feeling the tendency to employ a pattern of intellectual behaviors.

Sensitivity: Perceiving opportunities for, and appropriateness of, employing the pattern of behaviors.

Capability: Possessing the basic skills and capacities to carry through with the behaviors.

Commitment: Constantly striving to reflect on and improve performance of the pattern of intellectual behaviors.

Policy: Making it a policy to promote and incorporate the patterns of intellectual behaviors into actions, decisions, and resolutions of problematic situations.

HABITS OF MIND IN RELATION TO OTHER PROGRAMS AND PERSPECTIVES

Educators are constantly being admonished to implement a range of programs: whole language, accountability, integrated curriculum, character education, thematic instruction, school to work, and standards of performance, to mention only a few. Are the habits of mind yet another fad, another addition to an already overcrowded curriculum, or a replacement for what you are already doing? We think not. We believe they transcend these piecemeal, transient attempts to improve education.

We are witnessing an educational refocusing away from teaching unrelated, fragmented, short-term content toward broader, more enduring, essential, life-span learnings. Lauren Resnick (1999) states in her article, "Making America Smarter: The Real Goal of School Reform":

> For over 20 years, psychologists and other students of the human mind have been experimenting with ways of teaching the cognitive skills associated with intelligence. These include techniques as varied as generating analogies, making logical deductions, creating and using memory aids, and monitoring one's own state of knowledge (metacognition). Early experiments on teaching specific, isolated components of intelligence yielded a common pattern of results: Most of the training was successful in producing immediate gains in performance, but people typically ceased using the cognitive techniques they had been taught as soon as the specific conditions of training were removed. In other words, they became capable of performing whatever skill was taught, but they acquired no general habit of using it or capacity to judge for themselves when it was useful.
>
> As a result of these findings, cognitive researchers began to shift their attention to educational strategies that immerse students in demanding, long-term intellectual environments. Now positive results are coming in. In experimental programs and in practical school reforms, we are seeing that students who, over an extended period of time, are treated as if they are intelligent, actually become so.

Thus, the habits of mind fit within a pattern of educational trends and programs that share a common philosophy of teaching toward broader, more panoramic, encompassing and lifelong learning. Understanding the habits of mind in relationship to other educational programs and innovations would be helpful. While these relationships are explored in depth in Chapter 4, as well as throughout the four volumes in this series, following are some initial descriptions of the habits of mind in relation to various and specific educational innovations and efforts that share this philosophy of curriculum. These books, The Habits of Mind: A Developmental Series, take the next steps of implementation of this philosophy by providing many practical strategies, suggestions and experiences for shifting our educational focus toward this more expansive view of educational outcomes.

Habits of Mind and Dimensions of Learning

Dimension 5 in the Dimensions of Learning Program (Marzano, 1992, pp. 131–152) is entitled "Productive Habits of Mind," and it is considered one of the significant dimensions. The habits of mind that are named in Marzano's book are similar to the ones developed here and in the other books in this series.

For example, Marzano (1992) identifies the following habits of mind:

Self-Regulation
- Being aware of your own thinking.
- Planning.
- Being aware of necessary resources.
- Being sensitive to feedback.
- Evaluating the effectiveness of your actions.

Critical Thinking
- Being accurate and seeking accuracy.
- Being clear and seeking clarity.
- Being open minded.
- Resisting impulsivity.
- Taking and defending a position.
- Being sensitive to others.

Creative Thinking
- Engaging intensely in tasks even when answers or solutions are not immediately apparent.
- Pushing the limits of your knowledge and ability.
- Generating, trusting, and maintaining your own standards of evaluation.
- Generating new ways of viewing situations outside the boundaries of standard convention (pp. 138–139).

In Habits of Mind: A Developmental Series, we have provided rich examples of how to activate, engage, cultivate, and make the habits of mind a reality in the classroom, school system, and community at large.

Habits of Mind and the Coalition of Essential Schools

In the Coalition of Essential Schools, many schools have adopted habits of mind as a frame for their most essential outcomes. For example, at Central

Park East in New York City, their curriculum, instruction, and assessments are guided by the following central questions:

- From whose viewpoint is this? From what angle or perspective?
- How do we know when we know?
- What is the evidence and how reliable is it?
- How are things, events, people connected to each other?
- What is the cause and effect?
- How do they fit together?
- What's new and what's old?
- Have we run across this idea before?
- So what? Why does it matter? What does it mean?

To answer those questions, students must have well-developed habits of mind, such as applying past knowledge to new situations, striving for accuracy, and persisting. These habits of mind can be taught directly to students so they will have the disposition to struggle with the essential questions being asked.

HABITS OF MIND AND TECHNOLOGY

In her book *In the Age of the Smart Machine,* Zuboff (1988) refers to the "intellective skills" that are necessary for a computer-mediated work environment. She suggests that to work successfully as a "knowledge worker," a person will need the skills described in Figure 1.2.

As we consider the habits of mind, we can see that they are the necessary behaviors that will allow us to interact successfully in a computer-mediated environment. We will need to learn to listen with understanding and empathy, think flexibly, apply past knowledge to new situations, strive for accuracy, and question and pose problems. All the habits of mind introduced in this book are central to creating the productive work environment of the Information Age.

HABITS OF MIND AND THINKING SKILLS AND STRATEGIES

The past 10 years have seen a strong emphasis on infusing thinking skills into curriculum and instruction (Costa, 1991). How do habits of mind relate to thinking skills? After years of implementing both habits of mind and the Swartz and Parks infusing thinking model (Swartz & Parks, 1994), Mary Anne Kiser (personal communication, July 1999), principal of Meadow Glens Elementary School in Naperville, Illinois, describes the relationship between the two:

Intelligently behaving individuals are capable of thinking skillfully. Therein lies the power of the connection between the notion of intelligent behaviors, or habits of mind, and the model of infusion of thinking skills into classroom instruction. The habits provide the fuel to engage in strategic, skillful thinking. In order to skillfully engage in problem solving, decision making, analyzing assumptions, or checking the reliability of sources, one must possess the ability to decrease impulsivity, display empathy, and demonstrate inquisitiveness and persistence. The thinking behaviors/habits of mind provide the dispositions necessary to do the skillful thinking required by the infusion model within and beyond the classroom walls.

FIGURE 1.2

Desirable Skills

Problem Solving. This skill refers to the ability to work out problems as they occur. People will need to be able to abstract information from multiple sources of data from different databases and figure out how to make sense from the relationships, trends, and patterns.

Construction of Meaning. Workers will be required to use both inductive and deductive reasoning to apply a conceptual framework to the information they receive. For example, in education, teachers will have access to data about students from multiple databases. They will have to search for meaning as they see attendance records, tests and other assessment data, classroom instruction, curriculum in which students have participated in learning, and longitudinal information about the student as a learner in various disciplines. That sort of information has been in the system, but soon technological solutions will make available multiple data sources that can be retrieved for information about individual students. Then, the teacher will become key to the process of "making sense of the data."

Understanding Symbolic Representations. This skill refers to understanding materials such as graphs, charts, and diagrams. People will need the ability to understand abstract forms of representation and to interpret those abstractions as a part of constructing knowledge.

Collaboration. Problem solving is best done as a team because it requires "talk out loud" suggestions, experiments, and perspectives. In addition, with the advent of electronic text, people will be able to modify and interact with one another's work. When, for example, a teacher puts an idea out on the intra-net in a district, other teachers can interact with that idea online. Ideas can build, change, and grow in stature on the basis of these interactions.

We describe the relationship of habits of mind, cognitive operations, and thinking skills as hierarchical, as represented in Figure 1.3.

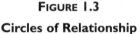

FIGURE 1.3

Circles of Relationship

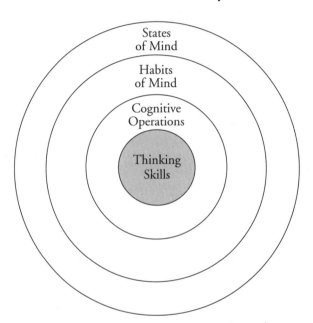

Being successful in school, at work, and in life depends upon acquiring and performing certain basic, discrete *thinking skills*, such as recalling, comparing, classifying, inferring, generalizing, evaluating, experimenting, and analyzing. According to Barry Beyer (1997), Edward de Bono (1991), and Reuven Feuerstein (Feuerstein et al., 1980), these skills may need to be taught directly.

Such skills, however, are seldom performed in isolation. Few people simply go out and observe, compare, or synthesize. Cognitive skills are engaged within a larger context in response to some stimulus. They are organized into and employed in combinations and sequences, which we refer to as *cognitive operations*, such as problem solving and decision making (Swartz & Parks, 1994; Ennis, 1991). Operations are larger strategies employed over time, and they require and include clusters of numerous cognitive skills. For example, decision making may require several cognitive skills: observing accurately, inferring causality, prioritizing, comparing and contrasting alternative choices, predicting consequences, and deducing.

Even though a person may have these skills and operational capacities, she must also be alert to opportunities in which they may be employed and, furthermore, have the inclination to employ them in an appropriate situation. To perform a *habit of mind*, therefore, requires more than possessing these basic skills and capacities to carry through with the behaviors. We believe that the habits of mind also encompass inclinations, proclivities, and characterizations.

Furthermore, we envision a larger, more encompassing, and complex level beyond the habits of mind. The performance and growth of the habits of mind are determined by the balance and strength of internal drives, forces, or passions referred to as *states of mind*: the invisible, internal human energy sources that motivate and drive human will. They give rise to and fuel dispositions, operations, and skills (Costa & Garmston, 1998). Examples of these states of mind include human beings' innate desire for reciprocity and human interaction, the drive for mastery and efficacy, innate curiosity and desire for exploration, and the remarkable capacity for adaptation.

HABITS OF MIND AND BRAIN RESEARCH

The recent explosion of neuroscientific research and its accompanying technology have vastly increased our understanding of how the brain works. Although we must be careful about educational interpretations and generalizations about brain research, we are beginning to see some support for engaging the habits of mind, particularly managing impulsivity, thinking interdependently, applying past knowledge to new situations, gathering data through all senses, and responding with wonderment and awe (Wolfe & Brandt, 1998).

Marian Diamond (Diamond & Hopson, 1998) describes some attributes of an enriched environment for children's intellectual development:

- A steady source of positive emotional support.
- Stimulation of all the senses (but not necessarily all at once).
- An atmosphere free of undue pressure and stress but suffused with a degree of pleasurable intensity.
- Novel challenges that are neither too easy nor too difficult for the child at the child's stage of development.
- Social interaction for a significant percentage of activities.
- Active participation rather than passive observation.
- Development of a broad range of skills and interests: mental, physical, aesthetic, social, and emotional.

Daniel Goleman (1995), who draws on the research of many other neuroscientists, suggests that managing the human impulse through building self-awareness, empathy, and social skills is the most basic form of intelligence and should become the purpose of education. Lawrence Lowery (1998) reminds us that the brain depends on having prior knowledge and is constantly constructing new relationships out of existing knowledge. As knowledge about how the brain works expands, we hope to gather further support for teaching the habits of mind.

HABITS OF MIND AND SCHOOL RESTRUCTURING

We believe that the most critical, but least understood, component of restructuring in the school reform movement is curriculum restructuring. Curriculum drives everything else. Curriculum is the pulse of the school; it is the currency through which educators exchange thoughts and ideas with students and the school community. It is the passion that binds the organization together.

Current reform movements are being driven by national, state, and local mandates; reorganization of time for the school day or the school year; redistribution of the power of decision-making processes; investments in technology; and recombinations of interdisciplinary teams and subjects. These and other such reforms constitute the "how" of delivery, not the sum and substance of what a school is all about.

When we begin to address the very heart of the organization, the curriculum, then all other reform efforts will fall into place. We have been building new reform structures around old-fashioned curriculum. Habits of Mind: A Developmental Series offers a bold proposal: Redesign the curriculum as the main component of restructuring the school.

We offer the habits of mind as a principle around which student learning, classrooms, schools, districts, and communities can be organized. The habits provide a congruent set of behaviors that pervade all levels of the organization. The habits of mind are as beneficial for adults in the community as they are for students. All of us can continue to develop these intelligent behaviors throughout our lifetimes. They are the covenants that can bind the organization together. The time is right for such a shift in thinking about how we educate.

HABITS OF MIND AND MULTIPLE INTELLIGENCES

Many teachers and schools that are focused on enhancing cognition have incorporated both Gardner's multiple intelligences and the habits of mind.

Although the habits of mind relate closely to the multiple intelligences (as well as Goleman's emotional intelligence), subtle differences do exist. The combination of the theories creates a powerful model.

Gardner's work describes a person's unique capacities to process information and represent knowledge. The habits of mind describe the propensity, inclination, and desire to employ certain dispositions while engaging in that processing of information. Those who excel in one or more of the multiple intelligences also have the propensity to draw upon one or more of the habits of mind. Here are examples:

• *Verbal Intelligence.* Surely listening with understanding and empathy, thinking and communicating with clarity and precision, striving for accuracy, and responding with wonderment and awe to words and their forms characterize such creative people as Toni Morrison, Ernest Hemingway, William Shakespeare, and Maya Angelou.

• *Kinesthetic Intelligence.* Like all dancers who reach the pinnacle of performance, Mikhail Baryshnikov must persist, strive for accuracy, and remain open to continuous learning. Olympic Gold Medalist Greg Louganis had to think about his thinking as he described how he would envision his body moving with style, grace, and precision before he dived off the board.

• *Musical Intelligence.* Persisting and striving for accuracy dominate this intelligence. Also included are creating, imagining, and innovating; listening with understanding and empathy; and thinking flexibly. It is said that Mozart was capable of creating and holding in his head an entire score (metacognition). Beethoven had to use senses other than hearing to compose his music. Both had to draw upon their creative resources.

• *Intrapersonal Intelligence.* Thinking about thinking (metacognition) is the prime habit here. Also included are thinking flexibly, listening with understanding and empathy, and responding with wonderment and awe. These habits were Carl Rogers's, Abraham Maslow's, and Milton Erickson's forte.

• *Interpersonal Intelligence.* Would not listening with understanding and empathy, thinking flexibly, thinking and communicating with clarity and precision, and questioning and posing problems be the hallmark of this intelligence? Interpersonally gifted people persevere even in conflicting, tense situations; they are fascinated with the power of altruism and cooperative efforts. Mother Teresa is a prime example.

• *Logical/Mathematical Intelligence.* Einstein, the archetype of this intelligence, also is characterized by his creativity and insight, his questioning, and his wonderment and awe. His capacity to imagine problems from different perspectives underscores his flexible thinking. Scientists and mathematicians who come to conclusions impulsively or make generalizations that are too broad would be criticized for their lack of scientific reasoning.

• *Spatial Intelligence.* Michelangelo made 100 renderings of a single hand before he was satisfied to paint it on the ceiling of the Sistine Chapel. This in itself is a portrait of persisting and striving for accuracy. Artists also must use thinking flexibly; creating, imagining, innovating; and applying past knowledge to new situations.

• *Naturalistic Intelligence* (Gardner, 1999). The keen observer of the natural world excels in the habits of questioning and posing problems, responding with wonderment and awe, and gathering data through all senses. Standing in awe of the beauty of a sunset, being charmed by the opening of a spring bud, being fascinated with the geometrics of a spider web—these habits would characterize such naturalist exemplars as John James Audubon, John Muir, and Charles Darwin.

Taken as a whole, the many definitions and interpretations of what is meant by intelligence leads us to conclude that habits of mind can be cultivated, articulated, operationalized, taught, fostered, modeled, and assessed. We need to so such work if we truly are to be guided by the rhetoric "all kids can learn." We need to modify that slogan to "all kids can learn *but not on the same day and not in the same way.*" Then, we have to understand what it means not only to say that phrase but also to operationalize it in classrooms.

The evidence is overwhelming. We can and must teach for higher levels of thinking. We can and must help students identify with the need to think with greater flexibility, wonderment, and ingenuity. This effort requires a new frame of mind, a new conception of what constitutes intelligence, and a paradigm shift about the role of schools and the education process. We can no longer be satisfied with a system that is willing to classify, categorize, and sort students on the basis of misaligned test scores. We have a responsibility to bring about a change in what it means to educate in a society that wants to value knowledge, informed decision making, and an equal opportunity for work and meaningful leisure. Habits of Mind: A Developmental Series is intended to encourage and support that change of mind.

REFERENCES

Beyer, B. (1997). *Improving student thinking: A comprehensive approach.* Boston, MA: Allyn & Bacon.

Coles, R. (1997). *The moral intelligence of children: How to raise a moral child.* New York: Random House.

Costa, A. (Ed.) (1991). *Developing minds: A resource book for teaching thinking* (Rev. ed., Vol. 1). Alexandria, VA: Association for Supervision and Curriculum Development.

Costa, A., & Garmston, R. (1998, October). Five human passions. *Think: The Magazine on Critical and Creative Thinking,* pp. 14–17.

de Bono, E. (1991). The CoRT thinking program. In A. Costa (Ed.), *Developing minds: Programs for teaching thinking* (Rev. ed., Vol. 2, pp. 27–32). Alexandria, VA: Association for Supervision and Curriculum Development.

Diamond, M., & Hopson, J. (1998). *Magic trees of the mind: How to nurture your child's intelligence, creativity, and healthy emotions from birth through adolescence* (pp. 107–108). New York: Penguin/Putnam.

Ennis, R. (1991). Goals for a critical thinking curriculum. In A. Costa (Ed.), *Developing minds: A resource book for teaching thinking* (Rev. ed., Vol. 1, pp. 68–71). Alexandria, VA: Association for Supervision and Curriculum Development.

Feuerstein, R., Rand, Y., Hoffman, M. B., & Miller, R. (1980). *Instrumental enrichment: An intervention program for cognitive modifiability.* Baltimore, MD: University Park Press.

Fogarty, R. (1997). *Brain compatible classrooms.* Arlington Heights, IL: Skylight Training and Publishing.

Gardner, H. (1983). *Frames of mind: The theory of multiple intelligences.* New York: BasicBooks.

Gardner, H. (1999, July). Multiple intelligences. Speech delivered at the Thinking for a Change Conference: 7th International Thinking Conference, Edmonton, Alberta, Canada.

Glatthorn, A., & Baron, J. (1991). The good thinker. In A. Costa (Ed.), *Developing minds: A resource book for teaching thinking* (Rev. ed., Vol. 1, pp. 63–67). Alexandria, VA: Association for Supervision and Curriculum Development.

Goleman, D. (1995). *Emotional intelligence: Why it can matter more than IQ.* New York: Bantam Books.

Gould, S. J. (1981). *The mismeasure of man.* New York: W. W. Norton.

Guilford, J. P., & Hoeptner, R. (1971). *The analysis of intelligence.* New York: McGraw-Hill.

Kotulak, R. (1997). *Inside the brain: Revolutionary discoveries of how the mind works.* Kansas City, MO: Andrews McMeel.

Lowery, L. (1998, November). How new science curriculums reflect brain research. *Educational Leadership, (56)*3, 26–30.

Machado, L. A. (1980). *The right to be intelligent.* New York: Pergamon Press.

Marzano, R. J. (1992). *A different kind of classroom: Teaching with Dimensions of Learning.* Alexandria, VA: Association for Supervision and Curriculum Development.

Perkins, D. (1991). What creative thinking is. In A. Costa (Ed.), *Developing minds: A resource book for teaching thinking* (Rev. ed., Vol. 1, pp. 85–88). Alexandria, VA: Association for Supervision and Curriculum Development.

Perkins, D. N. (1995). *Outsmarting IQ: The emerging science of learnable intelligence.* New York: The Free Press.

Resnick, L. B. (1999, June 16). Making America smarter. *Education Week*, pp. 38–40.

Resnick, L., & Hall, M. (1998, Fall). Learning organizations for sustainable education reform. *DAEDALUS: Journal of the American Academy of Arts and Sciences*, 89–118.

Sternberg, R. (1983). *How can we teach intelligence?* Philadelphia, PA: Research for Better Schools.

Sternberg, R. J. (1984). *Beyond I.Q.: A triarchic theory of human intelligence.* New York: Cambridge University Press.

Sternberg, R. J., Torff, B., & Grigorenko, E. (1998, May). Teaching for successful intelligence raises school achievement. *Phi Delta Kappan, 79*(9), 667–669.

Swartz, R., & Parks, S. (1994). *Infusing the teaching of critical and creative thinking into content instruction.* Pacific Grove, CA: Critical Thinking Press and Software.

Whimbey, A., Whimbey, L. S., & Shaw, L. (1975). *Intelligence can be taught.* New York: Lawrence Erlbaum Associates.

Wolfe, P., & Brandt, R. (1998, November). What do we know from brain research? *Educational Leadership, (56)*3, 8–13.

Zuboff, S. (1988). *In the age of the smart machine: The future of work and power.* New York: BasicBooks.

2

DESCRIBING THE
HABITS OF MIND

ARTHUR L. COSTA

When we no longer know what to do we have come to our real work and when we no longer know which way to go we have begun our real journey. The mind that is not baffled is not employed. The impeded stream is the one that sings.

Wendell Berry

This chapter contains descriptions for 16 attributes of what human beings do when they behave intelligently. In Habits of Mind: A Developmental Series, we choose to refer to them as habits of mind. They are the characteristics of what intelligent people do when they are confronted with problems, the resolutions to which are not immediately apparent.

These habits of mind seldom are performed in isolation; rather, clusters of behaviors are drawn forth and employed in various situations. For example, when listening intently, you employ the habits of thinking flexibly, thinking about thinking (metacognition), thinking and communicating with clarity and precision, and perhaps even questioning and posing problems.

Do not conclude, based on this list, that humans display intelligent behavior in only 16 ways. The list of the habits of mind is not complete. We want this list to initiate a collection of additional attributes. In fact, 12 attributes of "Intelligent Behavior" were first described in 1991 (Costa, 1991). Since then, through collaboration and interaction with many others, the list has been expanded. You, your colleagues, and your students will want to continue the search for additional habits of mind to add to this list of 16.

PERSISTING

Success seems to be connected with action. Successful people keep moving. They make mistakes but they never quit.

Conrad Hilton

Efficacious people stick to a task until it is completed. They don't give up easily. They are able to analyze a problem, and they develop a system, structure, or strategy to attack it. They have a repertoire of alternative strategies for problem solving, and they employ a whole range of these strategies. They collect evidence to indicate their problem-solving strategy is working, and if one strategy doesn't work, they know how to back up and try another. They recognize when a theory or idea must be rejected and another employed. They have systematic methods for analyzing a problem, which include knowing how to begin, what steps must be performed, and what data must be generated or collected. Because they are able to sustain a problem-solving process over time, they are comfortable with ambiguous situations.

Students often give up when the answer to a problem is not immediately known. They sometimes crumple their papers and throw them away exclaiming, "I can't do this!" or "It's too hard!" Sometimes they write down *any* answer to get the task over with as quickly as possible. Some of these students have attention deficits. They have difficulty staying focused for any length of time; they are easily distracted; or they lack the ability to analyze a problem and develop a system, structure, or strategy of attack. They may give up because they have a limited repertoire of problem-solving strategies, and thus they have few alternatives if their first strategy doesn't work.

MANAGING IMPULSIVITY

Goal-directed, self-imposed delay of gratification is perhaps the essence of emotional self-regulation: the ability to deny impulse in the service of a goal, whether it be building a business, solving an algebraic equation, or pursuing the Stanley Cup.

Daniel Goleman

Effective problem solvers are deliberate: They think before they act. They intentionally establish a vision of a product, action plan, goal, or destination before they begin. They strive to clarify and understand directions, they develop a strategy for approaching a problem, and they withhold immediate value judgments about an idea before they fully understand it. Reflective individuals consider alternatives and consequences of several possible directions before they take action. They decrease their need for trial and error by gathering information, taking time to reflect on an answer before giving it, making sure they understand directions, and listening to alternative points of view.

Often, students blurt out the first answer that comes to mind. Sometimes they shout an answer, start to work without fully understanding the directions, lack an organized plan or strategy for approaching a problem, or make immediate value judgments about an idea (criticizing or praising it) before they fully understand it. They may take the first suggestion given or operate on the first idea that comes to mind rather than consider alternatives and the consequences of several possible directions.

LISTENING WITH UNDERSTANDING AND EMPATHY

Listening is the beginning of understanding. . . . Wisdom is the reward for a lifetime of listening. Let the wise listen and add to their learning and let the discerning get guidance.

Proverbs 1:5

Highly effective people spend an inordinate amount of time and energy listening (Covey, 1989). Some psychologists believe that the ability to listen to another person—to empathize with and to understand that person's point of view—is one of the highest forms of intelligent behavior. The ability to paraphrase another person's ideas; detect indicators (cues) of feelings or emotional states in oral and body language (empathy); and accurately express another person's concepts, emotions, and problems—all

23

are indicators of listening behavior. (Piaget called it "overcoming egocentrism.")

People who demonstrate this habit of mind are able to see through the diverse perspectives of others. They gently attend to another person, demonstrating their understanding of and empathy for an idea or feeling by paraphrasing it accurately, building upon it, clarifying it, or giving an example of it.

Senge and his colleagues (1994) suggest that to listen fully means to pay close attention to what is being said beneath the words. You listen not only to the "music" but also to the essence of the person speaking. You listen not only for what someone knows but also for what that person is trying to represent. Ears operate at the speed of sound, which is far slower than the speed of light the eyes take in. Generative listening is the art of developing deeper silences in yourself, so you can slow your mind's hearing to your ears' natural speed and hear beneath the words to their meaning.

We spend 55 percent of our lives listening, but it is one of the least taught skills in schools. We often say we are listening, but actually we are rehearsing in our head what we are going to say when our partner is finished. Some students ridicule, laugh at, or put down other students' ideas. They interrupt, are unable to build upon, can't consider the merits of, or don't operate on another person's ideas.

We want students to learn to devote their mental energies to another person and to invest themselves in their partner's ideas. We want students to learn to hold in abeyance their own values, judgments, opinions, and prejudices so they can listen to and entertain another person's thoughts. This is a complex skill requiring the ability to monitor one's own thoughts while at the same time attending to a partner's words. Listening in this way does not mean we can't disagree with someone. Good listeners try to understand what other people are saying. In the end, they may disagree sharply, but because they have truly listened, they know exactly the nature of the disagreement.

THINKING FLEXIBLY

Of all forms of mental activity, the most difficult to induce even in the minds of the young, who may be presumed not to have lost their flexibility, is the art of handling the same bundle of data as before, but placing them in a new system of relations with one another by giving them a different framework, all of which virtually means putting on a different kind of thinking-cap for the moment. It is easy to teach anybody a new fact. . . . but it needs light from heaven above to enable a teacher to break the old framework in which the student is accustomed to seeing.

Arthur Koestler

An amazing discovery about the human brain is its plasticity—its ability to "rewire," change, and even repair itself to become smarter. Flexible people have the most control. They have the capacity to change their minds as they receive additional data. They engage in multiple and simultaneous outcomes and activities, and they draw upon a repertoire of problem-solving strategies. They also practice style flexibility, knowing when thinking broadly and globally is appropriate and when a situation requires detailed precision. They create and seek novel approaches, and they have a well-developed sense of humor. They envision a range of consequences.

Flexible people can approach a problem from a new angle using a novel approach, which de Bono (1991) refers to as "lateral thinking." They consider alternative points of view or deal with several sources of information simultaneously. Their minds are open to change based on additional information, new data, or even reasoning that contradicts their beliefs. Flexible people know that they have and can develop options and alternatives. They understand means-ends relationships. They can work within rules, criteria, and regulations, and they can predict the consequences of flouting them. They understand immediate reactions, but they also are able to perceive the bigger purposes that such constraints serve. Thus, flexibility of mind is essential for working with social diversity, enabling an individual to recognize the wholeness and distinctness of other people's ways of experiencing and making meaning.

Flexible thinkers are able to shift through multiple perceptual positions at will. One perceptual orientation is what Jean Piaget called egocentrism, or perceiving from our own point of view. By contrast, allocentrism is the position in which we perceive through another person's orientation. We operate from this second position when we empathize with another's feelings, predict how others are thinking, and anticipate potential misunderstandings.

Another perceptual position is macrocentric. It is similar to looking down from a balcony to observe ourselves and our interactions with others. This bird's-eye view is useful for discerning themes and patterns from assortments of information. It is intuitive, holistic, and conceptual. Because we often need to solve problems with incomplete information, we need the

25

capacity to perceive general patterns and jump across gaps of incomplete knowledge.

Yet another perceptual orientation is microcentric, examining the individual and sometimes minute parts that make up the whole. This worm's-eye view involves logical, analytical computation, searching for causality in methodical steps. It requires attention to detail, precision, and orderly progressions.

Flexible thinkers display confidence in their intuition. They tolerate confusion and ambiguity up to a point, and they are willing to let go of a problem, trusting their subconscious to continue creative and productive work on it. Flexibility is the cradle of humor, creativity, and repertoire. Although many perceptual positions are possible—past, present, future, egocentric, allocentric, macrocentric, microcentric, visual, auditory, kinesthetic—the flexible mind knows when to shift between and among these positions.

Some students have difficulty considering alternative points of view or dealing with more than one classification system simultaneously. *Their* way to solve a problem seems to be the *only* way. They perceive situations from an egocentric point of view: "My way or the highway!" Their minds are made up: "Don't confuse me with facts. That's it!"

THINKING ABOUT THINKING (METACOGNITION)

When the mind is thinking it is talking to itself.

Plato

Occurring in the neocortex, metacognition, or thinking about thinking, is our ability to know what we know and what we don't know. It is our ability to plan a strategy for producing what information is needed, to be conscious of our own steps and strategies during the act of problem solving, and to reflect on and evaluate the productiveness of our own thinking. Although inner language, thought to be a prerequisite for metacognition, begins in most children around age 5, metacognition is a key attribute of formal thought flowering about age 11.

The major components of metacognition are developing a plan of action, maintaining that plan in mind over a period of time, and then reflecting on and evaluating the plan upon its completion. Planning a strategy before embarking on a course of action helps us keep track of the steps in the sequence of planned behavior at the conscious awareness level for the duration of the activity. It facilitates making temporal and comparative judgments; assessing the readiness for more or different activities; and monitoring our interpretations, perceptions, decisions, and behaviors. An example would be what superior teachers do daily: developing a teaching strategy for a lesson, keeping that strategy in mind throughout the instruction, and then reflecting upon the strategy to evaluate its effectiveness in producing the desired student outcomes.

Intelligent people plan for, reflect on, and evaluate the quality of their own thinking skills and strategies. Metacognition means becoming increasingly aware of one's actions and the effect of those actions on others and on the environment; forming internal questions in the search for information and meaning; developing mental maps or plans of action; mentally rehearsing before a performance; monitoring plans as they are employed (being conscious of the need for midcourse correction if the plan is not meeting expectations); reflecting on the completed plan for self-evaluation; and editing mental pictures for improved performance.

Interestingly, not all humans achieve the level of formal operations (Chiabetta, 1976). As Russian psychologist Alexander Luria found, not all adults metacogitate (Whimbey, Whimbey, & Shaw, 1975). The most likely reason is that all of us do not take the time to reflect on our experiences. Students often do not take the time to wonder why they are doing what they are doing. They seldom question themselves about their own learning strategies or evaluate the efficiency of their own performance. Some children virtually have no idea of what they should do when they confront a problem, and often they are unable to explain their decision-making strategies (Sternberg & Wagner, 1982). When teachers ask, "How did you solve that problem? What strategies did you have in mind?" or "Tell us what went on in your head to come up with that conclusion," students often respond, "I don't know. I just did it."

We want students to perform well on complex cognitive tasks. A simple example might be drawn from a reading task. While reading a passage, we sometimes find that our minds wander from the pages. We see the words, but no meaning is being produced. Suddenly, we realize that we are not concentrating and that we've lost contact with the meaning of the text. We recover by returning to the passage to find our place, matching it with the last thought we can remember, and once having found it, reading on with connectedness. This inner awareness and the strategy of recovery are components of metacognition.

STRIVING FOR ACCURACY

A man who has committed a mistake and doesn't correct it is committing another mistake.

Confucius

Whether we are looking at the stamina, grace, and elegance of a ballerina or a shoemaker, we see a desire for craftsmanship, mastery, flawlessness, and economy of energy to produce exceptional results. People who value accuracy, precision, and craftsmanship take time to check over their products. They review the rules by which they are to abide, they review the models and visions they are to follow, and they review the criteria they are to use to confirm that their finished product matches the criteria exactly. To be craftsmanlike means knowing that one can continually perfect one's craft by working to attain the highest possible standards and by pursuing ongoing learning to bring a laser-like focus of energies to accomplishing a task.

These people take pride in their work, and they desire accuracy as they take time to check over their work. Craftsmanship includes exactness, precision, accuracy, correctness, faithfulness, and fidelity. For some people, craftsmanship requires continuous reworking. Mario Cuomo, a great speechwriter and politician, once said that his speeches were never done; it was only a deadline that made him stop working on them.

Some students may turn in sloppy, incomplete, or uncorrected work. They are more anxious to get rid of the assignment than to check it over for accuracy and precision. They are willing to settle for minimum effort rather than invest their maximum. They may be more interested in expedience rather than excellence.

QUESTIONING AND POSING PROBLEMS

The formulation of a problem is often more essential than its solution, which may be merely a matter of mathematical or experimental skill. . . .

*To raise new questions, new possibilities, to regard old problems from a
new angle, requires creative imagination and marks real advances.*

Albert Einstein

One of the distinguishing characteristics of humans is our inclination and
ability to *find* problems to solve. Effective problem solvers know how to ask
questions to fill in the gaps between what they know and what they don't
know. Effective questioners are inclined to ask a range of questions:

- What evidence do you have?
- How do you know that's true?
- How reliable is this data source?

They also pose questions about alternative points of view:

- From whose viewpoint are we seeing, reading, or hearing?
- From what angle, what perspective, are we viewing this situation?

Students pose questions that make causal connections and relationships:

- How are these (people, events, or situations) related to each other?
- What produced this connection?

Sometimes they pose hypothetical problems characterized by "if"
questions:

- What do you think would happen IF. . . ?
- IF that is true, then what might happen IF. . . ?

Inquirers recognize discrepancies and phenomena in their environment,
and they probe into their causes:

- Why do cats purr?
- How high can birds fly?
- Why does the hair on my head grow so fast, while the hair on my
  arms and legs grows so slowly?
- What would happen if we put the saltwater fish in a fresh water
  aquarium?
- What are some alternative solutions to international conflicts, other
  than wars?

Some students may be unaware of the functions, classes, syntax, or intentions in questions. They may not realize that questions vary in complexity, structure, and purpose. They may pose simple questions intending to derive maximal results. When confronted with a discrepancy, they may lack an overall strategy to search for and find a solution.

APPLYING PAST KNOWLEDGE TO NEW SITUATIONS

I've never made a mistake. I've only learned from experience.

Thomas A. Edison

Intelligent humans learn from experience. When confronted with a new and perplexing problem, they will draw forth experiences from their past. They often can be heard to say, "This reminds me of . . ." or "This is just like the time when I . . . ." They explain what they are doing now with analogies about or references to their experiences. They call upon their store of knowledge and experience as sources of data to support, theories to explain, or processes to solve each new challenge. They are able to abstract meaning from one experience, carry it forth, and apply it in a novel situation.

Too often, students begin each new task as if it were being approached for the first time. Teachers are dismayed when they invite students to recall how the students solved a similar problem previously—and students don't remember. It's as if they had never heard of it before, even though they recently worked with the same type of problem! It seems each experience is encapsulated and has no relationship to what has come before or what comes after. Their thinking is what psychologists refer to as an "episodic grasp of reality" (Feuerstein, Rand, Hoffman, & Miller, 1980); that is, each event in life is separate and discrete, with no connections to what may have come before or with no relation to what follows. Their learning is so encapsulated that they seem unable to draw forth from one event and apply it in another context.

THINKING AND COMMUNICATING WITH CLARITY AND PRECISION

I do not so easily think in words. . . . after being hard at work having arrived at results that are perfectly clear. . . . I have to translate my thoughts in a language that does not run evenly with them.

Francis Galton, Geneticist

Language refinement plays a critical role in enhancing a person's cognitive maps and their ability to think critically, which is the knowledge base for efficacious action. Enriching the complexity and specificity of language simultaneously produces effective thinking.

Language and thinking are closely entwined; like either side of a coin, they are inseparable. Fuzzy language is a reflection of fuzzy thinking. Intelligent people strive to communicate accurately in both written and oral form, taking care to use precise language; defining terms; and correct names, labels, and analogies. They strive to avoid overgeneralizations, deletions, and distortions. Instead, they support their statements with explanations, comparisons, quantification, and evidence.

We sometimes hear students and other adults using vague and imprecise language. They describe objects or events with words like *weird, nice,* or *okay.* They name specific objects using such nondescriptive words as *stuff, junk,* and *things.* They punctuate sentences with meaningless interjections like *ya know, er,* and *uh.* They use vague or general nouns and pronouns: " *They* told me to do it!", " *Everybody* has one!", or " *Teachers* don't understand me." They use nonspecific verbs: "Let's *do* it." At other times, they use unqualified comparatives: "This soda is *better,* I like it *more.*"

GATHERING DATA THROUGH ALL SENSES

Observe perpetually.

Henry James

The brain is the ultimate reductionist. It reduces the world to its elementary parts: photons of light, molecules of smell, sound waves, vibrations of touch—all of which send electrochemical signals to individual brain cells that store information about lines, movements, colors, smells, and other sensory inputs.

Intelligent people know that all information gets into the brain through sensory pathways: gustatory, olfactory, tactile, kinesthetic, auditory, and visual. Most linguistic, cultural, and physical learning is derived from the environment by observing or taking it in through the senses. To know a wine it must be drunk; to know a role it must be acted; to know a game it must be played; to know a dance it must be moved; to know a goal it must be envisioned. Those whose sensory pathways are open, alert, and acute absorb more information from the environment than those whose pathways are withered, immune, and oblivious to sensory stimuli.

We are learning more and more about the impact of arts and music on improved mental functioning. Forming mental images is important in mathematics and engineering; listening to classical music seems to improve spatial reasoning. Social scientists use scenarios and role-playing; scientists build models; engineers use CAD-CAM; mechanics learn through hands-on experimentation; artists explore colors and textures; and musicians combine instrumental and vocal music.

Some students, however, go through school and life oblivious to the textures, rhythms, patterns, sounds, and colors around them. Sometimes children are afraid to touch or get their hands dirty. Some don't want to feel an object that might be slimy or icky. They operate within a narrow range of sensory problem-solving strategies, wanting only to "describe it but not illustrate or act it," or to "listen but not participate."

CREATING, IMAGINING, INNOVATING

The future is not some place we are going to but one we are creating. The paths are not to be found, but made, and the activity of making them changes *both the maker and the destination.*

John Schaar, Political Scientist

All human beings have the capacity to generate novel, clever, or ingenious products, solutions, and techniques—*if* that capacity is developed. Creative human beings try to conceive problem solutions differently, examining alternative possibilities from many angles. They tend to project themselves into different roles using analogies, starting with a vision and working backward, and imagining they are the object being considered. Creative people take risks and frequently push the boundaries of their perceived limits (Perkins, 1991). They are intrinsically rather than extrinsically motivated, working on the task because of the aesthetic challenge rather than the material rewards.

Creative people are open to criticism. They hold up their products for others to judge, and they seek feedback in an ever-increasing effort to refine their technique. They are uneasy with the status quo. They constantly strive for greater fluency, elaboration, novelty, parsimony, simplicity, craftsmanship, perfection, beauty, harmony, and balance.

Students, however, often are heard saying, "I can't draw," "I was never very good at art," "I can't sing a note," or "I'm not creative." Some people believe creative humans are just born that way and that "it's in those humans' genes and chromosomes."

RESPONDING WITH WONDERMENT AND AWE

The most beautiful experience in the world is the experience of the mysterious.

Albert Einstein

Describing the 200 best and brightest of *USA Today's* All USA College Academic Team, Tracey Wong Briggs (1999) states, "They are creative thinkers who have a passion for what they do." Efficacious people have not only an "I can" attitude but also an "I enjoy" feeling. They seek problems to solve for themselves and to submit to others. They delight in making up problems to solve on their own, and they so enjoy the challenge of problem solving that they seek perplexities and puzzles from others. They enjoy figuring things out by themselves, and they continue to learn throughout their lifetimes.

Some children and adults avoid problems and are turned off to learning. They make such comments as, "I was never good at these brain teasers," "Go ask your father; he's the brain in this family," "It's boring,"

"When am I ever going to use this stuff?", "Who cares?", "Lighten up, Teacher. Thinking is hard work," or "I don't do thinking!" Many people never enrolled in another math class or other "hard" academic subjects after they didn't have to in high school or college. Many people perceive thinking as hard work, and they recoil from situations that demand too much of it.

We want students to be curious, to commune with the world around them, to reflect on the changing formations of a cloud, to feel charmed by the opening of a bud, to sense the logical simplicity of mathematical order. Students can find beauty in a sunset, intrigue in the geometric shapes of a spider web, and exhilaration in the iridescence of a hummingbird's wings. They can see the congruity and intricacies in the derivation of a mathematical formula, recognize the orderliness and adroitness of a chemical change, and commune with the serenity of a distant constellation. We want them to feel compelled, enthusiastic, and passionate about learning, inquiring, and mastering.

TAKING RESPONSIBLE RISKS

There has been a calculated risk in every stage of American development—the pioneers who were not afraid of the wilderness, businessmen who were not afraid of failure, dreamers who were not afraid of action.

Brooks Atkinson

Flexible people seem to have an almost uncontrollable urge to go beyond established limits. They are uneasy about comfort; they live on the edge of their competence. They seem compelled to place themselves in situations where they do not know what the outcome will be. They accept confusion, uncertainty, and the higher risks of failure as part of the normal process, and they learn to view setbacks as interesting, challenging, and growth producing. However, they do not behave impulsively. Their risks are educated. They draw on past knowledge, are thoughtful about consequences, and have a well-trained sense of what is appropriate. They know that all risks are not worth taking.

Risk taking can be considered in two categories: those who see it as a *venture* and those who see it as *adventure*. The venture part of risk taking might be described in terms of what a venture capitalist does. When a person is approached to take the risk of investing in a new business, she will look at the markets, see how well organized the ideas are, and study the economic projections. If she finally decides to take the risk, it is a well-considered one.

The adventure part of risk taking might be described by the experiences from project adventure. In this situation, there is a spontaneity, a willingness to take a chance in the moment. Once again, a person will take the chance only if experiences suggest that the action will not be life threatening or if that person believes that group support will protect the person from harm. (Checking out the dimensions of weight, distance, strength, and guarantees of a bungee cord before agreeing to the exhilaration of the drop, for example.) Ultimately, people learn from such high-risk experiences that they are far more able to take actions than they previously believed. Risk taking becomes educated only through repeated experiences. It often is a cross between intuition, drawing on past knowledge, striving for precision and accuracy, and a sense of meeting new challenges.

Bobby Jindal, executive director of the National Bipartisan Commission on the Future of Medicare, states, "The only way to succeed is to be brave enough to risk failure" (Briggs, 1999, p. 2A). When people hold back from taking risks, they miss opportunities. Some students seem reluctant to take risks. Some students hold back from games, new learning, and new friendships because their fear of failure is far greater than their desire for venture or adventure. They are reinforced by the mental voice that says, "If you don't try it, you won't be wrong," or "If you try it and you are wrong, you will look stupid." The other voice that might say, "If you don't try it, you will never know," is trapped by fear and mistrust. These students are more interested in knowing whether their answer is correct or not, rather than being challenged by the process of finding the answer. They are unable to sustain a process of problem solving and finding the answer over time, and therefore they avoid ambiguous situations. They have a need for certainty rather than an inclination for doubt.

We hope that students will learn how to take intellectual as well as physical risks. Students who are capable of being different, going against the grain of common thinking, and thinking of new ideas (testing them with peers and teachers) are more likely to be successful in an age of innovation and uncertainty.

FINDING HUMOR

Where do bees wait? At the buzz stop.

Andrew, Age 6

Another unique attribute of human beings is our sense of humor. Its positive effects on psychological functions include a drop in the pulse rate, secretion of endorphins, and increased oxygen in the blood. Humor has been found to liberate creativity and provoke such higher-level thinking skills as anticipating, finding novel relationships, visual imaging, and making analogies. People who engage in the mystery of humor have the ability to perceive situations from an original and often interesting vantage point. They tend to initiate humor more often, to place greater value on having a sense of humor, to appreciate and understand others' humor, and to be verbally playful when interacting with others. Having a whimsical frame of mind, they thrive on finding incongruity; perceiving absurdities, ironies, and satire; finding discontinuities; and being able to laugh at situations and themselves.

Some students find humor in all the wrong places—human differences, ineptitude, injurious behavior, vulgarity, violence, and profanity. They laugh at others yet are unable to laugh at themselves. We want student to acquire this characteristic of creative problem solvers so they can distinguish between situations of human frailty and fallibility that need compassion and those that truly are funny (Dyer, 1997).

THINKING INTERDEPENDENTLY

Take care of each other. Share your energies with the group. No one must feel alone, cut off, for that is when you do not make it.

Willie Unsoeld, Renowned Mountain Climber

Humans are social beings. We congregate in groups, find it therapeutic to be listened to, draw energy from one another, and seek reciprocity. In groups we contribute our time and energy to tasks that we would quickly tire of when working alone. In fact, solitary confinement is one of the cruelest forms of punishment that can be inflicted on an individual.

Cooperative humans realize that all of us together are more powerful, intellectually or physically, than any one individual. Probably the foremost disposition in the postindustrial society is the heightened ability to think in concert with others, to find ourselves increasingly more interdependent and sensitive to the needs of others. Problem solving has become so complex that no one person can go it alone. No one has access to all the data needed to make critical decisions; no one person can consider as many alternatives as several people.

Some students may not have learned to work in groups; they have underdeveloped social skills. They feel isolated, and they prefer solitude. They say things like, "Leave me alone—I'll do it by myself!" "They just don't like me!" or "I want to be alone." Some students seem unable to contribute to group work and are job hogs; conversely, other students let all the others in a group do all the work.

Working in groups requires the ability to justify ideas and to test the feasibility of solution strategies on others. It also requires developing a willingness and openness to accept feedback from a critical friend. Through this interaction, the group and the individual continue to grow. Listening, consensus seeking, giving up an idea to work with someone else's, empathy, compassion, group leadership, knowing how to support group efforts, altruism—all are behaviors indicative of cooperative human beings.

REMAINING OPEN TO CONTINUOUS LEARNING

Insanity is continuing to do the same thing over and over and expecting different results.

Albert Einstein

Intelligent people are in a continuous learning mode. Their confidence, in combination with their inquisitiveness, allows them to constantly search for new and better ways. People with this habit of mind are always striving for improvement, growing, learning, and modifying and improving themselves.

They seize problems, situations, tensions, conflicts, and circumstances as valuable opportunities to learn.

A great mystery about humans is that many times we confront learning opportunities with fear rather than mystery and wonder. We seem to feel better when we know rather than when we learn. We defend our biases, beliefs, and storehouses of knowledge rather than invite the unknown, the creative, and the inspirational. Being certain and closed gives us comfort, while being doubtful and open gives us fear.

Thanks to a curriculum employing fragmentation, competition, and reactiveness, students from an early age are trained to believe that deep learning means figuring out the truth rather than developing capabilities for effective and thoughtful action. They have been taught to value certainty rather than doubt, to give answers rather than to inquire, to know which choice is correct rather than to explore alternatives.

Our wish is for creative students and people who are eager to learn. The habit of mind includes the humility of knowing that we don't know, which is the highest form of thinking we will ever learn. Paradoxically, unless you start off with humility, you will never get anywhere. As the first step, you must already have what eventually will be the crowning glory of all learning: to know—and to admit—that you don't know and to not be afraid to find out.

THE RIGHT STUFF

The beautiful thing about learning is that nobody can take it away from you.

B. B. King

The 16 habits of mind you've just considered were drawn from research on human effectiveness, descriptions of remarkable performers, and analyses of the characteristics of efficacious people. These habits of mind can serve as mental disciplines. When confronted with problematic situations, students, parents and teachers might habitually employ one or more of these habits of mind by asking themselves, "What is the most *intelligent* thing I can do right now?" They also might consider these questions:

• How can I learn from this? What are my resources? How can I draw on my past successes with problems like this? What do I already know about the problem? What resources do I have available or need to generate?

• How can I approach this problem flexibly? How might I look at the situation in another way? How can I draw upon my repertoire of problem-solving strategies? How can I look at this problem from a fresh perspective (lateral thinking)?

• How can I illuminate this problem to make it clearer, more precise? Do I need to check out my data sources? How might I break this problem down into its component parts and develop a strategy for understanding and accomplishing each step?

• What do I know or not know? What questions do I need to ask? What strategies are in my mind now? What am I aware of in terms of my own beliefs, values, and goals with this problem? What feelings or emotions am I aware of that might be blocking or enhancing my progress?

• How does this problem affect others? How can *we* solve it together? What can I learn from others that would help me become a better problem solver?

Community organizer Saul Alinsky coined a very useful slogan: "DON'T JUST DO SOMETHING . . . STAND THERE!" Taking a reflective stance in the midst of active problem solving is often difficult. For that reason, each of these habits of mind is situational and transitory. There is no such thing as perfect realization of any of them. They are utopian states toward which we constantly aspire. Csikszentmihalyi (1993) states, "Although every human brain is able to generate self-reflective conscious-ness, not everyone seems to use it equally" (p. 23). Few people, notes Kegan (1994), ever *fully* reach the stage of cognitive complexity, and rarely before middle age.

These habits of mind transcend all subject matters commonly taught in school. They are characteristic of peak performers in all places: homes, schools, athletic fields, organizations, the military, governments, churches, or corporations. They are what make marriages successful, learning contin-ual, workplaces productive, and democracies enduring. The goal of educa-tion, therefore, should be to support ourselves and others in liberating, developing, and habituating these habits of mind more fully. Taken togeth-er, they are a force directing us toward increasingly authentic, congruent, and ethical behavior. They are the touchstones of integrity and the tools of disciplined choice making. They are the primary vehicles in the lifelong journey toward integration. They are the "right stuff" that make human beings efficacious.

REFERENCES

Briggs, T. W. (1999, February 25). Passion for what they do keeps alumni on first team. *USA Today, 17*(115), pp. 1A–2A.

Chiabetta, E. L. A. (1976). Review of Piagetian studies relevant to science instruction at the secondary and college levels. *Science Education 60,* 253–261.

Costa, A. (1991). The search for intelligent life. In A. Costa (Ed.), *Developing minds: A resource book for teaching thinking* (Rev. ed., Vol. 1, pp. 100–106). Alexandria, VA: Association for Supervision and Curriculum Development.

Covey, S. (1989). *The seven habits of highly effective people: Powerful lessons in personal change.* New York: Simon and Schuster.

Csikszentmihalyi, M. (1993). *The evolving self: A psychology for the third millennium.* New York: HarperCollins.

de Bono, E. (1991). The CoRT thinking program. In A. Costa (Ed.), *Developing minds: Programs for teaching thinking* (Rev. ed., Vol. 2, pp. 27–32). Alexandria, VA: Association for Supervision and Curriculum Development.

Dyer, J. (1997). Humor as process. In A. Costa and R. Liebmann (Eds.), *Envisioning process as content: Toward a renaissance curriculum* (pp. 211–229). Thousand Oaks, CA: Corwin Press.

Feuerstein, R., Rand, Y., Hoffman, M. B., & Miller, R. (1980). *Instrumental enrichment: An intervention program for cognitive modifiability.* Baltimore, MD: University Park Press.

Kegan, R. (1994). *In over our heads: The mental complexity of modern life.* Cambridge, MA: Harvard University Press.

Perkins, D. (1991). What creative thinking is. In A. Costa (Ed.), *Developing minds: A resource book for teaching thinking* (Rev. ed., Vol. 1, pp. 85–88). Alexandria, VA: Association for Supervision and Curriculum Development.

Senge, P. M., Roberts, C., Ross, R. B., Smith, B. J., & Kleiner, A. (1994). *The fifth discipline fieldbook: Strategies and tools for building a learning organization.* New York: Doubleday/Currency.

Sternberg, R., & Wagner, R. (1982). *Understanding intelligence: What's in it for education?* Paper submitted to the National Commission on Excellence in Education.

Whimbey, A., Whimbey, L. S., & Shaw, L. (1975). *Intelligence can be taught.* New York: Lawrence Erlbaum Associates.

WHY TEACH
HABITS OF MIND?

SHARI TISHMAN

Now, what I want is, Facts. Teach these boys and girls nothing but Facts. Facts alone are wanted in life. Plant nothing else, and root out everything else. You can only form the minds of reasoning animals upon Facts; nothing else will ever be of any service to them.

Charles Dickens, Hard Times

The quotation above is spoken by Mr. Gradgrind, the stern schoolmaster in Dickens's novel of the Industrial Revolution. Mr. Gradgrind surely believes that his educational philosophy is as enlightened as the new mood of the 19th century: Stoke the furnace of the mind with facts, and out will grind knowledge! Yet we know, as Dickens knew, that a view of schooling based on the grim, dehumanizing procedures of industrialization is a poor model for teaching and learning. This model historically has influenced education, but most educators have moved toward an emphasis on person-centered skills and abilities. Unlike Mr. Gradgrind, we now want to teach students *how* to do things, not just what to know.

Depending on our educational goals, the skills and abilities we aim to teach run the gamut from basic literacy skills to vocational skills to discipline-based skills to broad critical and creative-thinking skills. In recent years, some educators have broadened this skill-centered view of learning into a more dispositional view. This view emphasizes the teaching of broad, high-level intellectual behaviors. Such behaviors include skills, but they also encompass attitudes, motivations, emotions, and other elements typically left out of a skill-centered view of learning.

Different writers have suggested slightly different lists of top-10 intellectual behaviors, alternatively labeling them habits of mind, as they are called in this book and series, or thinking dispositions (Ennis, 1987; Facione, Sanchez, Facione, & Gainen, 1995; Perkins, Jay, & Tishman, 1993). Despite the different appellations, the lists are quite similar in spirit. By and large, they all emphasize curiosity, flexibility, posing problems, decision making, being reasonable, creativity, risk taking, and other behaviors that support critical and creative thought. Characteristic of all these lists is a respect for people's abilities to make their own informed choices and to direct their own intellectual behaviors.

The habits of mind view is a theory of education, a philosophy of what and how people should learn. Like any theory of education, it rests on a foundation of beliefs and values. An age-old tool for exploring such foundations is philosophical examination—the practice of critically probing assumptions and beliefs to see what they rest on and whether they are justified. Schopenhauer (1970), a philosopher famous for his no-holds-barred critical spirit, says that the two main requirements for philosophical examination are "firstly, to have the courage not to keep any question back; and secondly, to attain a clear consciousness of anything that goes without saying so as to comprehend it as a problem" (p. 117). This advice is very much in the spirit of habits of mind, and it serves as a good guide for exploring them. This chapter discusses four fundamental features of habits of mind that, taken together, suggest a persuasive answer to the chapter's central question: Why teach habits of mind?

HONORING TEMPERAMENT AND DIFFERENCES

Character is a long-standing habit.

Plutarch

Education is about helping people develop and exercise their intelligence, and a philosophy of education can't help but take at least a tacit stand on the question of what intelligence is made of. Most traditional views of intelligence emphasize the cognitive skills that people are capable of demonstrating upon demand. Certainly, cognitive skill is important, but let's apply the second piece of Schopenhauer's advice and try to "attain a clear consciousness of anything that goes without saying so as to comprehend it as a problem."

What goes without saying in the ability-centered view of intelligence is the belief that there is a direct and dependable link between ability and action. In other words, it is a belief that simply having an ability to think in a certain way pretty much guarantees that one will do so. Yet people possess all kinds of abilities that they don't use, or they don't use appropriately.

For example, many people have the capacity to make thoughtful decisions, but they aren't motivated to do so. Many people know how to pose problems and ask questions, but frequently they don't see the purpose in it. Many people have the ability to be persistent, but they lack the will or the inclination. Many people have the ability to think empathically, but they don't see it as a valuable part of learning.

Abilities alone are dry and dormant. Passions, motivation, sensitivities, and values all play a role in bringing intelligent behavior to life. Defining intelligence as a matter of ability, without honoring all the other elements that enliven it, fails to capture its human spark. The habits of mind express a character-centered view of intelligence that honors the role of temperament and individual differences. In contrast to an ability-centered view, the habits of mind view intelligence as dispositional. A disposition is a propensity to act in a certain way. Viewing intelligence dispositionally says that intelligence is expressed as characteristic patterns of intellectual behavior in everyday situations.

If developing students' intelligence involves cultivating specific habits of mind, are not individuality and individual differences threatened? Doesn't it say, in effect, that all good thinkers will or should have the same personality and the same intellectual profile? Not at all. Character is much broader than personality. For example, consider self-reflectiveness, part of the metacognitive habit of thinking about thinking. This character trait manifests itself differently in different individuals. A person can be deeply self-reflective, obsessively self-reflective, or tentatively self-reflective. Or consider the habit of persistence. Some people are doggedly persistent, others are strategically persistent, some are quietly persistent, others are intensely persistent, and still others are foolishly persistent. Character traits are like broad physical traits: They can be shared by many people and yet look quite different in different individuals. Most everyone has a pair of eyes, but very few pairs of eyes look alike.

The habits of mind also honor individual differences by emphasizing broad character traits that aren't tied to a single modality or intelligence. For example, flexibility can be exercised verbally, kinesthetically, or musically. Persistence can be applied to activities in virtually every modality. Questions can be posed in words, in images, through music, and through movement. Far from limiting individuality of expression, the habits of mind encourage it.

MAKING ROOM FOR EMOTION

The connection between emotions and intelligence has received a good deal of attention in recent years. Many views of education now explicitly recognize the importance of emotions, or emotional intelligence, and the habits of mind are no different. The habits of mind make room for the many roles of emotion in intelligence. Sometimes, however, the various ways that emotions contribute to thinking go unexamined. Because different emotions affect thinking in different ways, it's worth taking a closer look at exactly how emotions are involved in the habits of mind.

Perhaps the most obvious way the habits of mind make room for emotions is by specifically naming inclination as an attribute of intelligent behavior. Inclination is a feeling of being drawn to or pulled by something, a desire for a certain outcome, or a drive to act in a certain way. Honoring the emotions connected with inclination follows naturally from a character-centered rather than skill-centered conception of intelligence. If intelligence is defined as how we truly feel inclined to think, not just how we are capable of thinking, then the feelings connected with inclination need to be part of our conception of intelligence.

Another two attributes of habits of mind that make room for emotion are a valuing of specific intellectual behaviors and a commitment to strive to continually reflect on and improve them. To value a pattern of intellectual behavior is to care about it. To make a commitment to strive to improve a pattern of behavior is to feel strongly about its importance.

The emotions involved in valuing and committing to intellectual behaviors like the habits of mind are reminiscent of what psychologist R. S. Peters (1974) calls the "rational passions." These are the emotionally charged beliefs and commitments that underlie the pursuit of knowledge. They include a passion for truth and truthfulness, a love of accuracy, and an abhorrence of intellectual dishonesty. These are genuine passions, like any others, because they are deeply felt and play a strong role in motivating behavior. Philosopher Israel Scheffler (1977) observes that rational passions contribute to intellectual conscience. Intellectual conscience exists in a deep concern for being as true as possible to reality and an equally deep discomfort with intellectual shoddiness and dishonesty. Without intellectual conscience, intelligence is blind. Although rational passions aren't habits of mind in the sense that persistence, problem posing, and metacognition are, they serve as the emotional compass that points these and similar intellectual behaviors in the right direction.

A third and rather different way that the habits of mind honor the role of emotions in intelligence is the emphasis on empathy. Rational passions may motivate the pursuit of knowledge. But sometimes, in a much stronger sense, knowing is feeling. Empathy is an imaginative taking-on of the feelings of another person, and it is literally a mode of understanding. To know something empathically is to know something through the faculty of feeling.

To include empathy as a top-level habit of mind—listening with understanding and empathy—makes an implicit claim about the nature of knowledge that should be clearly stated. The implicit claim is this: Sometimes, to know something is to feel it rightly. Consider coming to understand the experience of eastern European immigrants who arrived in New York City in the early years of the 20th century. Is it possible to know their story in a detached and objective way without experiencing any kindred or empathic feelings? Without somehow imaginatively feeling what it must have been like to enter a city in which every sound and sight were strange and overwhelming? In a very real sense, to understand something about this immigrant experience is to enter into the feeling of it.

To claim that feeling is a way of knowing departs from what sometimes has been called the standard scientific view of knowledge, which contends that knowledge is objective and can be apprehended purely intellectually. Most contemporary educators and philosophers no longer think this view is true, though it still lives on in many instructional and assessment practices.

Finally, a fourth way that the habits of mind honor the role of emotions is by emphasizing emotional self-management. To act on one's intellectual values and commitments and to choose certain patterns of behavior over others, even in the face of countervailing forces, involve emotional self-control, resourcefulness, and insight. Writers such as Daniel Goleman (1995) have helped publicize the importance of emotional self-management in intelligent behavior. The habits of mind are compatible with this view, emphasizing self-reflection, managing impulsivity, and persisting.

ATTENDING TO "SENSITIVITY"

One of the quieter but perhaps most significant features of the habits of mind is the recognition of the importance of intellectual sensitivity. The habits of mind draw explicit attention to sensitivity, which is an important and much overlooked element of intelligent behavior. Sensitivity involves the perception or recognition of opportunities to appropriately engage in certain patterns of intellectual behavior. For example, it involves recognizing opportunities to think flexibly, to ask questions, to listen with empathy, or to be self-reflective.

The claim that sensitivity is important is like a wolf in sheep's clothing. It appears to be a mild and self-evident point: Who would argue with the notion that it's important to notice occasions to think? But this apparent mildness hides something that, as Schopenhauer might put it, has "gone without saying" in traditional accounts of good thinking. Typically, when we think about cultivating students' intellectual behavior, we think of the problem as having two sides: ability and motivation, or skill and will. You need to teach the right intellectual skills, the story goes, but you also have to motivate students to use them. Sensitivity is taken for granted.

Motivation is important, of course, and so are intellectual skills. But research reveals that sensitivity plays a much larger role in effective thinking than one might expect. Students often have quite a bit of difficulty perceiving opportunities to think critically and creatively when these opportunities are embedded in the everyday stream of life, even when they possess the skills and the will to do so.

A series of studies conducted by David Perkins, myself, and other colleagues at Harvard Project Zero reveals some interesting phenomena concerning sensitivity. Here are three relevant findings:

• First, we learned that sensitivity can truly be distinguished empirically from ability and inclination in measures of intellectual performance. In other words, sensitivity appears to be a genuine component of intelligence in its own right, distinct from both ability and inclination.

• Second, by measuring the relative contribution of inclination, sensitivity, and ability to overall intellectual performance, we discovered that sensitivity is often more of a roadblock to good thinking than a failure of inclination. In other words, students often fail to do their best thinking not because they aren't able to, and not because they don't want to, but *because they simply don't recognize occasions to do so.*

• Third, sensitivity is not as strongly correlated with IQ as is ability. In other words, high scores on ability measures are not necessarily accompanied by high scores on sensitivity measures. The reverse also is true: High scores on sensitivity measures don't necessarily reflect high ability. This finding underscores a belief that many educators already have. Traditional intelligence measures such as IQ tests (and standardized tests, whose scores are highly correlated with IQ) don't tell the whole story of intelligent behavior.

Earlier I mentioned that the emphasis on sensitivity as a component of good thinking is a wolf-like claim in sheep's clothing. Part of its wolfishness consists in the rather daunting challenge of finding ways to teach sensitivity, which is very different from teaching skills or inspiring motivation. Teaching sensitivity means teaching students to notice, on their own, opportunities to employ habits of mind. Such work involves teaching students to notice occasions when it is appropriate to ask questions rather than pointing these occasions out to them. It involves teaching students to perceive the need for persistence rather than telling them when to persist. It involves cultivating a sensitivity to the need for precision rather than admonishing students to be accurate.

Sensitivity is often triggered by emotions (Tishman, 1998). For example, sensitivity to occasions for asking questions is often cued by a feeling of puzzlement or curiosity: We feel puzzled and interpret the feeling as a cue to ask questions. But we can also interpret puzzlement as a signal to give up on an inquiry, to not bother asking questions and to throw in the towel. Similarly, feelings of confusion or frustration can be interpreted as cues to persist in an inquiry. But they also can be perceived as signals to give up. More subtly, perhaps, that itchy, impatient feeling of wanting to raise one's voice to get one's opinion heard can be a cue to do simply that and drown out others. Or it can be interpreted as a signal to try harder to listen to others. By emphasizing the importance of sensitivity, the habits of mind remind us that emotions need interpreting. How they are interpreted influences the direction of intellectual activity.

Although sensitivity often is cued by emotions, it is triggered in other ways, too. For example, psychologist Ellen Langer (1989) believes that our alertness to thinking occasions can be heightened by heightening our general state of mindfulness. In the research I mentioned earlier, we learned that the visual layout of text has a surprisingly strong influence on sensitivity. Researcher Ron Ritchhart is currently conducting research into the behaviors of effective teachers who successfully cultivate sensitivity, and early observations suggest that the visual text on the classroom wall— posters, quotes, and so on—plays an important role (Ritchhart, 1998). But these findings are just the beginning. Considerably more research into how to cultivate sensitivity is needed. Very few, if any, contemporary instructional philosophies acknowledge the role of sensitivity, and its inclusion in the attributes of habits of mind is a great strength.

CROSS-CONTEXT RELEVANCE

This chapter has discussed some broad theoretical features of habits of mind. But of course the habits of mind are more than abstract theory. The habits of mind emphasize broad intellectual behaviors that are relevant and important across disciplines and in everyday life.

For example, the habit of thinking flexibly, the ability to see things from diverse perspectives, is important when interpreting scientific evidence. It also is relevant to understanding works of art, to exploring the viewpoints of others, and in making the myriad life decisions students face as they mature. The habit of listening with understanding and empathy is relevant to literature and the arts; it also is important when evaluating philosophical arguments and envisioning scientific systems.

Let's consider cross-context relevance from two angles. First, are broad habits of mind really transferable across context? Second, are the habits of mind culturally justifiable? In the spirit of Schopenhauer, a good way to analyze a claim is to explore possible objections to it.

THE TRANSFERABILITY OBJECTION

Suppose we are convinced that the intellectual behaviors expressed by the habits of mind are indeed useful ways of gaining understanding in many different contexts. We still need to know whether they transfer across contexts, which is a somewhat different issue. Just because transferring, say, the habit of questioning and posing problems from science to the arts to the workplace and beyond would be efficacious doesn't mean that the mind obligingly works that way. Indeed, some scholars have argued that cognitive skills are deeply context bound (e.g., Lave, 1988). Basically, the argument goes like this: We learn cognitive skills within a very specific context. Even if a skill is theoretically applicable to a wide variety of situations, or even if the skill is obviously useful and relevant, it can be so tightly linked to the contextual cues of the discipline or to the context in which it was learned that we are blind to other opportunities to apply it. For example, you may learn to pose good scientific problems in the context of the science lab, but that skill doesn't predict anything about your propensity to pose problems elsewhere.

There are two factors to remember. First, the tendency to transfer is itself a habit of mind. In this book, it goes by the label "applying past knowledge to new situations." Some people appear to have a greater propensity than others to seek wide applicability for the knowledge and skills they learn. The skills of transfer can also be taught (see Bransford, Franks, Vye, & Sherwood, 1989; Fogarty, Perkins, & Barell, 1991; Perkins & Salomon, 1988). For example, people can be taught to look for comparisons between learning in one context and learning in another, and to seek cross-disciplinary connections.

A second point concerning the transferability of habits of mind is that they express a *dispositional* view of intelligence that goes beyond basic cognitive capacity to include character traits, values, and emotions, including the sensitivity to interpret emotions and other stimuli as cognitive cues. So one way the habits of mind account for the problem of transfer is by proposing that dispositions, rather than skills, are the "stuff" that is generalized across contexts. This view certainly has a good deal of theoretical support. As mentioned in the beginning of this chapter, many researchers and educators have conceptualized good thinking as a matter of a small set of broadly generalized thinking dispositions. A limited amount of empirical research has been conducted that explores the generality of these dispositional aspects of intelligence, by and large with positive results (Facione et al., 1995; Perkins & Tishman, 1997; Stanovich & West, 1997). More research is needed. A long research tradition in personality psychology shows that although acknowledging the interaction between personality and situational variables is important, some broad personality traits *do* tend to be quite stable across a wide range of situations (traits such as extroversion and introversion, timidity, adventuresomeness, flexibility, and achievement orientation). We cannot, however, automatically assume that habits of mind will have the same sort of stability profile. But the research does suggest that, if one is looking for broad transfer across contexts, taking a character-centered rather than skill-centered view of intellectual behavior makes more sense.

THE CULTURAL BIAS OBJECTION

A second objection to claiming broad relevance for habits of mind concerns their cultural orientation. Behaviors such as flexibility, persistence, and reasonableness may be well and good for students who live in families and communities that value them, but what about students who don't? We can't escape the fact that virtually any list of educational goals will reflect cultural ideals. We live inside a culture, and we can't help but value those behaviors that we believe best suit its philosophy or worldview. This is as true for habits of mind as any other view. But one dimension of habits of mind is worth inspecting more closely. This dimension concerns the connection to critical thinking.

Many of the habits of mind discussed in this book and elsewhere have been put forth as intellectual behaviors that support critical thinking. We have often heard that the teaching of critical thinking is especially suitable for a democratic culture because it is the best training for informed and intelligent democratic citizenship. But we have also heard that in certain authoritarian cultures, the critical spirit—which includes asking questions, probing assumptions, and seeking reasons—is *not* a valued disposition. When students who live within these cultures at home encounter critical thinking in school, the experience can cause distress. Certainly, educators need to be sensitive to the connection between the classroom culture and the culture of the home. But no classroom anywhere will perfectly mirror the culture of each child's home, and the question of whether there should be a parallel between the home culture and the culture of the classroom is different than the question of whether habits of mind that support critical thinking have a cultural bias.

The philosopher Robert Ennis has carefully examined this question, and proposes an interesting and compelling answer. He defines critical thinking as "thinking that is reasonable and reflective, and is focused on deciding what to believe or do" (Ennis, 1998, p. 16). He argues that critical thinking is *not* biased (i.e., it is objectively worthwhile) for any culture that values decision making that best achieves the culture's goals or ideals. His point is that the decisions that are most likely to achieve a culture's goals are best made "if seeking reasons and alternatives, and being open to alternatives[,] are part of the activity" (Ennis, 1998, p. 30).

In other words, decision makers in any culture that wants to preserve itself (which is pretty much any culture one can think of) do their job best when they think critically about the decisions they make. This view does not take a stand on whether the culture's goals are correct or incorrect, morally right or morally wrong. Nor does it take a stand on whether all members of the culture are, or should be, decision makers. These issues are cultural matters. What's at stake is whether or not to teach students the skills and dispositions that will empower them to be decision makers within their own cultures. This is a choice that individual educators and families have to make. Those who do not want their students or children to be empowered to make decisions for themselves will do well to avoid habits of mind.

A HUMANISTIC PHILOSOPHY

Questions often spiral back to themselves, and as we conclude, this chapter returns to the question with which it began: Why teach habits of mind? I have suggested that the following four features of the habits of mind are significant:

• The habits of mind are based on a character-centered view of intelligence that emphasizes attitudes, habits, and character traits in addition to cognitive skill.

• The habits encompass a view of thinking and learning that accommodates several of the different roles that emotions play in good thinking.

• The habits of mind recognize the importance of sensitivity, which is a key yet often-overlooked feature of intelligent behavior.

• The habits are a set of specific intellectual behaviors that support critical and creative thought within, across, and beyond school subjects.

Mr. Gradgrind would be disappointed with what he read in this chapter. The habits of mind view is not a philosophy of facts. It is a humanistic philosophy of respect for others that expresses a belief in people's capacity for developing their intellect through reasoned reflection and appropriate emotion. Why teach the habits of mind? At this point, I invite you to decide for yourself.

REFERENCES

Bransford, J. D., Franks, J. J., Vye, N. J., & Sherwood, R. D. (1989). New approaches to instruction: Because wisdom can't be told. In S. Vosniadou & A. Ortony (Eds.), *Similarity and analogical reasoning.* New York: Cambridge University Press.

Ennis, R. H. (1987). A taxonomy of critical thinking dispositions and abilities. In J. B. Baron & R. S. Sternberg (Eds.), *Teaching thinking skills: Theory and practice* (pp. 9–26). New York: W. H. Freeman.

Ennis, R. H. (1998). Is critical thinking culturally biased? *Teaching Philosophy, 21*(1), 15–33.

Facione, P. A., Sanchez, C. A., Facione, N. C., & Gainen, J. (1995). The disposition toward critical thinking. *Journal of General Education, 44*(1), 1–25.

Fogarty, R., Perkins, D. N., & Barell, J. (1991). *How to teach for transfer.* Palatine, IL: Skylight Training and Publishing.

Goleman, D. (1995). *Emotional intelligence: Why it can matter more than IQ.* New York: Bantam Books.

Langer, E. (1989). *Mindfulness.* Reading, MA: Addison-Wesley.

Lave, J. (1988). *Cognition in practice: Mind, mathematics, and culture in everyday life.* New York: Cambridge University Press.

Perkins, D. N., Jay, E., & Tishman, S. (1993). Beyond abilities: A dispositional theory of thinking. *The Merrill-Palmer Quarterly, 39*(1), 1–21.

Perkins, D. N., & Salomon, G. (1988, September). Teaching for transfer. *Educational Leadership, 46*(1), 22–32.

Perkins, D., & Tishman, S. (1997, July 14–16). *Intelligence and personality: Bridging the gap in theory and measurement.* Paper presented at The Second Spearman Seminar, The University of Plymouth, Devon, England.

Peters, R. S. (1974). *Psychology and ethical development.* London: Allen & Unwin.

Ritchhart, R. (1998). *Developing intellectual character: Six case studies of teachers' enculturative practice.* Unpublished doctoral dissertation proposal. Harvard University Graduate School of Education, Cambridge, MA.

Scheffler, I. (1977). In praise of the cognitive emotions. *Teachers College Record 79*(2), 171–186.

Schopenhauer, A. (1970). *Essays and aphorisms.* Penguin: New York.

Stanovich, K. E., & West, R. F. (1997). Reasoning independently of prior belief and individual differences in actively open-minded thinking. *Journal of Educational Psychology, 89*(2), 342–357.

Tishman, S. (1998, October). Metacognitive emotion and metacognitive knowledge. *THINK Magazine,* 7–10.

HABITS OF MIND
IN THE CURRICULUM

ARTHUR L. COSTA AND BENA KALLICK

Whenever educators set about transforming schools, they often begin with the question of curriculum. The work of Heidi Hayes Jacobs suggests that it is powerful to begin an examination of curriculum through "curriculum mapping" (Jacobs, 1997). In this process, teachers detail what they currently teach and consider how it rests on the shoulders of previous and future years. At the same time, they consider what might be excessive, repetitious, necessary, or missing.

Jacobs suggests that the entire faculty engage in this process, not just a small committee. Curriculum mapping provides a rich opportunity for building curriculum as a decision-making process. The power of these conversations comes from the four basic groups of decisions that teachers consider:

- Deciding on outcomes, goals, intentions, and purposes.
- Deciding on content, strategies, and skills.
- Deciding on materials, resources, and organizational patterns.
- Deciding on measures of student learning.

These decisions about what should be taught, how it should be taught, and how it should be assessed shape the minds of all children. The character of their minds, in turn, helps shape the culture in which we all live. Eliot Eisner (1997) states that schools serve children best when they help students broaden their understanding of content in meaningful ways. We

Note: Many of the ideas presented in this chapter are drawn from the article "Maturing Outcomes" by Arthur L. Costa and Robert J. Garmston, which was published in _Encounter: Education for Meaning and Social Justice,_ Vol. 11, No. 1. Spring, 1998.

suggest that to achieve this goal, habits of mind must be considered among all the varying curriculum goals and outcomes.

In this chapter, we present a systemic map of increasingly broader levels of curricular outcomes. We believe children need to shape and give meaning to their learning in as broad a context as possible. Our hope is to offer all students a curriculum that is developed around broad outcomes and focused on enduring, essential, transdisciplinary learnings that are as appropriate for adults as they are for students. These learnings should also be congruent with a vision of continuous, lifelong learning and with the mission of a learning organization.

BROAD EDUCATIONAL OUTCOMES

Anthropologist Gregory Bateson (1972) formulated an early notion of relating systems of learning to human growth. Dilts (1994) then applied this form of systems thinking to education. The major concepts are as follows:

1. Any system of activity is a subsystem embedded inside of another system. This system also is embedded in an even larger system, and so on.

2. Learning in one subsystem produces a type of learning relative to the system in which one is operating.

3. The effect of each level of learning is to organize and control the information on the level below it.

4. Learning something on an upper level will change things on lower levels, but learning something on a lower level may or may not inform and influence levels above it.

These insights led to a realization that authentic outcomes are subsystems embedded inside other subsystems. In such arrangements, different types and magnitudes of learning occur relative to the system in which one operates. Each more overarching, complex, and abstract level has a greater impact upon the learning of the level within it. Because each level affects the interpretation of the levels below, changing meaning on an upper level changes decisions and actions at lower levels; changing something at a lower level, however, does not necessarily affect the upper levels.

When educators make decisions about curriculum, instructional methodologies, and assessment strategies, they hold in their minds at least four nested levels of outcomes. Each one is broader and more encompassing than the level within, and each represents greater authenticity. These levels are summarized in Figure 4.1, and they are detailed in the text below.

FIGURE 4.1

Four Levels of Outcomes

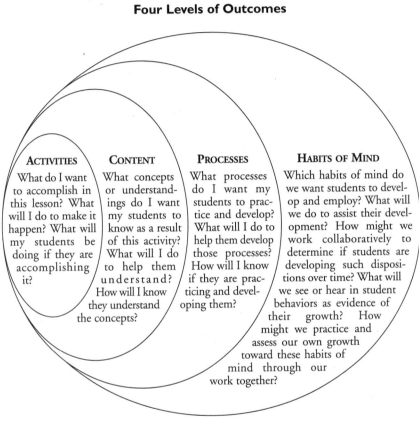

ACTIVITIES

What do I want to accomplish in this lesson? What will I do to make it happen? What will my students be doing if they are accomplishing it?

CONTENT

What concepts or understandings do I want my students to know as a result of this activity? What will I do to help them understand? How will I know they understand the concepts?

PROCESSES

What processes do I want my students to practice and develop? What will I do to help them develop those processes? How will I know if they are practicing and developing them?

HABITS OF MIND

Which habits of mind do we want students to develop and employ? What will we do to assist their development? How might we work collaboratively to determine if students are developing such dispositions over time? What will we see or hear in student behaviors as evidence of their growth? How might we practice and assess our own growth toward these habits of mind through our work together?

Source: Adapted from Costa & Liebmann, 1997.

OUTCOMES AS ACTIVITIES

Inexperienced teachers often exhibit episodic, teacher-centered thinking. They are satisfied simply to accomplish *activities*. For beginning teachers, for whom everything is new, the cognitive demands of the classroom can be more than the working mind is designed to accommodate. Their instructional choices are dictated by their own needs for survival and for keeping students engaged from period to period.

These teachers' decisions include: "What do I want to accomplish in this lesson? What will I do to make it happen? What will my students be doing if they are accomplishing it?" They then describe outcomes such as, "Today in social studies I'm going to show a videotape on Mexico." Success is measured in terms of: "Did I make it through the lesson? Were students on task? Did they learn something from the tape?"

OUTCOMES AS CONTENT

As teachers gain familiarity with classroom procedures, their students, and themselves, mental energy is freed to consider the cumulative effects of classroom activities: What concepts and principles are students learning? While teachers maintain interest in day-to-day activities, the activities are now employed as vehicles to learn content. Teachers ask: "What concepts or understandings do I want my students to know as a result of this activity? What will I do to help them understand? How will I know they understand the concepts?"

In the Mexican history lesson described earlier, for example, the videotape would be used as a means to help students understand the principal causes of Mexico's struggle for independence. The teacher focuses on what concepts and understandings students will know and how that knowledge will be recognized and assessed.

OUTCOMES AS PROCESSES

As teachers continue to mature, they begin to select content for its generative qualities (Perrone & Kallick, 1997). Content becomes a vehicle for experiencing, practicing, and applying the processes needed to think creatively and critically: observing and collecting data, formulating and testing hypotheses, drawing conclusions, and posing questions.

Process outcomes are of greater valence than the outcomes of subject-specific content because to be literate in the content, students must know and practice the processes by which that content came into being (Paul & Elder, 1994; Tishman & Perkins, 1997). At this level, teachers decide: "What processes do I want my students to practice and develop? What will I do to help them develop those processes? How will I know if they are practicing and developing them?"

In the Mexican history example, students might plan a research project to support their theories that the heroes of the Mexican Revolution were as courageous as those of the American Revolution. Students could present an exhibit demonstrating their understandings and develop rubrics for judging the exhibits and working together effectively. Additionally, they might reflect on and evaluate themselves both individually and collectively, considering how well they met criteria for the project's completion and for cooperative group work.

OUTCOMES AS HABITS OF MIND

With increased maturity, teachers view outcomes systemically. In other words, they see their outcomes in relation to the shared vision of the school community, and they understand the long-range, cumulative, enduring nature of learning. They understand that success is desired not only in school but also in life. When all staff members share this kind of vision, their work transcends grade levels and subject areas. Panoramic outcomes are more likely to be achieved because they are reinforced, transferred, and revisited throughout the school, at home, and in the community.

The transcendent qualities of systems thinking about outcomes can be found in such habits of mind as enhancing one's capacities for persisting; managing impulsivity; creating, imagining, innovating; thinking about thinking (metacognition); striving for accuracy; listening with understanding and empathy; taking responsible risks; and responding with wonderment and awe (Costa, 1991; Tishman & Perkins, 1997). All teachers, regardless of subject area or grade level, can agree on these desirable qualities. Persistence is as valued in social sciences as it is in music, math, and physical education. Creative thinking is as important to science as it is in the auto shop and the arts.

With a focus on habits of mind, the historical isolation, disparity, and episodic nature of curricular outcomes are minimized. Furthermore, these dispositions are as applicable to developing adult capacities for effective problem solving and continuous learning as they are to students. All members of the learning organization continue to become more thoughtful. The outcomes for students and the work culture of the school become congruent and synonymous.

It should be emphasized that activities are still taught. Content is selected for its generative nature, and processes are practiced, but they now accumulate into grander, more long-range outcomes. Activities, content, and process become vehicles for achieving the larger, more enduring, and essential habits of mind. Instead of a single teacher asking "What do I want?", instructional teams now decide: "Which habits of mind do we want students to develop and employ? What will we do to assist their development? How might we work collaboratively to determine if students are developing such dispositions over time? What will we see or hear in student behaviors as evidence of their growth? How might we practice and assess our own growth toward these habits of mind through our work together?"

In the Mexican history lesson, the teacher can build metacognitive capabilities by having students consciously discuss and employ the skills of listening with understanding and empathy. The teacher will guide students to generate operational definitions of these dispositions, and observers can collect evidence of the group's performance of these skills. Upon completion of the project, students might evaluate their own performance using feedback from the observers. Students can draw causal relationships not only among the effects of their collaborative skills and task achievement but also between empathy and the sources of revolutionary movements. They might be asked questions such as: "What metacognitive strategies did you employ to manage and monitor your listening skills during your work in teams?" The emphasis is on internalizing these dispositions as individual and community-wide norms, and all staff members plan for such dispositions to be encountered and transferred across various disciplines and learning situations.

Staff and students learn to draw upon the habits of mind to organize and direct their intellectual resources as they confront and resolve problems, observe human frailty in themselves and others, plan for the most productive interventions in groups, and search out the motivations of their own and other's actions. The habits become the desirable meta-outcomes for the entire community—staff and students.

The following letter from Peter King, a graduate of Smoky Hills High School in Aurora, Colorado, illustrates his transcendence to a more "panoramic view" of educational outcomes:

> In the packet I read about "intellects," it says that people who behave intelligently are great problem solvers who are not necessarily mathematicians or scientists. Some are people like mechanics. The skills it takes to be a good mechanic are all listed in this packet. And when I say that, I disgust myself in thinking that all mechanics are morons. I'm talking about how hypocritical it is to say that mechanics are stupid when I'm one myself. Everybody is a mechanic in a way, but me in particular because I've had industrial arts and automotive classes since 9th grade. My passion is fixing my car, making it go faster and better. So how could I think badly about mechanics? Well, it's that little thing known as peer pressure. My parents, friends, and a majority of people look down on people who fix cars. So, I look down on myself; I hide my hobby like it was a crime. People don't realize the massive amount of problem-solving power it takes to fix someone else's mess.
>
> All of these characteristics of intelligent behavior are used by "industrial artists." But don't get me wrong, there are definitely bad mechanics.

That's why I fix my car myself. I believe the same skills I use in my Critical Thinking/Discussion Class are the ones I use to diagnose an engineering problem:

• Persevering when the solution is not readily apparent. (It took me months to fix a vibration the car made that no other mechanic could fix.)
• Checking for Accuracy
• Problem Posing
• Working with Past Knowledge
• Ingenuity and Creativity (Ask Mr. Ferrari about this one!)

These I believe are the most-used skills. We are all "mechanics" in a way. It's just that some of us get our hands greasy.

When teachers deliberately adopt and assess habits of mind, it changes the design of their activities, determines their selection of content, and enlarges their assessments. The bigger the circle in which the outcomes live, the more influence they exert on the values of each learning (Meadows, 1997). If we wish to influence an element deeper within the system, each tiny adjustment in the environment surrounding it produces profound effects on the entire system. This realization allows us to search beyond the habits of mind for systems to which we naturally aspire in our journey of human development, which, if affected, also would influence our capacity to learn (Garmston, 1997).

BEYOND CURRENT THINKING

We've described four transcendent levels of maturing outcomes: from activities to content to processes to habits of mind. We hold each level not only as outcomes in and of themselves but as vehicles and enablers of more transcendent virtues as well. As the instructional focus is enlarged, student outcomes and the school work culture become congruent and synonymous. The staff employs these same habits of mind as they make their own decisions, plan instruction, and conduct meetings and parent conferences. Staff members monitor their own habits of mind as they gather feedback about their achievements and their effects on others, and they set continually higher standards for themselves.

Biographies of remarkable and virtuous people from the sciences, the arts, politics, and social services, whose personal development seemed to move beyond the habits of mind, further enlarge our vision. These people display a personal set of virtues, a spiritual quality. This next higher level might be referred to as "ideals"—encompassing not only the mastery of activities, content, processes, and habits of mind, but also transcending them in pursuit of universal goals. The real challenge to the maturing organization is not only to be faithful to the external goals but also to measure up to the interior goals. It is a challenge to reach for what is beautiful, what is good, what is true, and what unites and does not divide. We believe the ideal for which humans at the highest stages of development strive is the integration of external and internal outcomes. We all are trying to make ourselves better, purer, more beautiful; we all want to be more loving persons, concerned with uniting and not dividing (*Gifts from the Fire*, 1991).

REFERENCES

Bateson, G. (1972). *Steps to an ecology of mind.* San Francisco: Chandler.

Costa, A. (1991). The search for intelligent life. In A. Costa (Ed.), *The school as a home for the mind* (pp. 19–31). Palatine, IL: Skylight Training and Publishing.

Costa, A., & Liebmann, R. (1997). Toward a renaissance curriculum: An idea whose time has come. In A. Costa & R. Liebmann (Eds.), *Envisioning process as content: Toward a renaissance curriculum* (pp. 1–20). Thousand Oaks, CA: Corwin Press.

Dilts, R. (1994). *Effective presentation skills.* Capitola, CA: META Publications.

Eisner, E. (1997, January). Cognition and representation: A way to pursue the American dream? *Phi Delta Kappan, 78*(5), 348–353.

Garmston, R. (1997, Spring). Nested levels of learning. *Journal of Staff Development, (18)*2, 66–68.

Gifts from the Fire: The Ceramic Art of Brother Thomas [Videotape]. (1991). Boston, MA: Pucker Gallery.

Jacobs, H. H. (1997). *Mapping the big picture: Integrating curriculum and assessment K–12.* Alexandria, VA: Association for Supervision and Curriculum Development.

Meadows, D. (1997, Winter). Places to intervene in a system (in increasing order of effectiveness). *Whole Earth,* 79–83.

Paul, R., & Elder, L. (1994). All content has a logic: That logic is given by a disciplined mode of thinking, Part 1. *Teaching Thinking and Problem Solving, (16)*5, 1–4.

Perrone, V., & Kallick, B. (1997). Generative topics for process curriculum. In

A. Costa & R. Liebmann (Eds.), *Supporting the spirit of learning: When process is content* (pp. 23–24). Thousand Oaks, CA: Corwin Press.

Tishman, S., & Perkins, D. (1997, January). The language of thinking. *Phi Delta Kappan 78*(5), 368–374.

THE WORK ETHIC AND THE HABITS OF MIND

MARIAN LEIBOWITZ

More and more, schools are interacting with corporations and businesses through school-to-career apprenticeships. In the course of this work, educators hear employees in varied workplaces discuss their mission, their vision, and the ethic required to perform to the highest quality. It is common for these employees to use terms like "continuous improvement" and "learning organization." Likewise, in schools, teachers talk with students about the need to take greater responsibility for doing their work with care and quality, not just "get it done."

Among the many issues debated in U.S. education, we find universal agreement on at least one aspect of schooling: Students need to develop and demonstrate a stronger work ethic. Businesses seek self-directed workers. Educators seek "the good old days" when students cared about the quality of their work. Parents express concern about children's lack of responsibility. Society yearns for demonstrations of honesty, caring, and self-control. These concerns for a work ethic easily translate into the application of the habits of mind.

In this chapter, I explore connections between and among the workplace, its conception of a work ethic, and the habits of mind. I consider schools as a workplace and the need to instill a work ethic into curriculum, instruction, and assessment. I also examine how the habits of mind serve as leverage for this integration to take place.

WORKPLACE ETHICS

What is "the work ethic"? Both schools and businesses talk about self-direction, high-quality performance with self-assessment, self-management, and self-modification for continuous improvement. In an employee hand-book published by Pritchett & Associates, we find a call to

> Fully do your job. . . . There's no room for employees who mainly put in their time, going through the motions but giving only half-hearted effort. . . . In today's world, career success belongs to the committed. [It belongs to] those who work from the heart . . .[,] who invest themselves passionately in their jobs. . .[,] and who recommit quickly when change reshapes their work (Pritchett, 1994, p. 6).

The 1991 SCANS report calls for performance in addition to basic skills and thinking skills. It defines the performance:

Personal Qualities: Displays responsibility, self-esteem, sociability, self-management, and integrity and honesty.
   A. *Responsibility*—exerts a high level of effort and perseveres towards goal attainment.
   B. *Self-Esteem*—believes in own self-worth and maintains a positive view of self.
   C. *Sociability*—demonstrates understanding, friendliness, adaptability, empathy, and politeness in group settings.
   D. *Self-Management*—assesses self accurately, sets personal goals, monitors progress, and exhibits self-control.
   E. *Integrity/Honesty*—chooses ethical courses of action (U.S. Department of Labor, 1991, p. xviii).

The professional world outside schools requires demonstration of a work ethic and makes the need for this ethic visible to the public and employees. Organizations like Footlocker, United Airlines, and Summa Health Care Services make their expectations explicit, and they collect data to help monitor and modify employees' actions, leading to the demonstrations of desired skills. Often, the personal qualities of promptness, regulation, and punctuality are cited.

For example, the major corporation Footlocker expects the following from its employees (among a variety of other attributes):

- A *concern for effectiveness.* A desire to do the job better.
- *Initiative* to go beyond what the situation requires without being asked.
- *Enthusiasm* for work.
- *Self-confidence.*

Figure 5.1 shows how United Airlines, a corporation with a strong commitment to collaboration, delivers a clear message regarding expected behaviors. The halls of the United Airlines Reservation Center in Sterling, Virginia, are similar to an elementary school. Charts, posters, and bulletin boards are used to help collect and promote progress toward these and other goals. The building is filled with demonstrations of performance and a constant striving for greater quality. Figure 5.2 illustrates how Summa Health System details its employee expectations.

FIGURE 5.1

United Airlines "Rules of the Road"

We respect each other and listen with an open mind.

We trust each other.

We keep our commitments.

We speak with honesty and candor.

We reach and acknowledge closure on decisions.

We support and respect team decisions as our own.

We place team interests before our own.

We provide complete and impartial information.

We actively recognize and celebrate successes.

We address conflict with an individual directly, constructively, and confidentially.

We include the stakeholders in decisions.

We plan before we act.

We call each other on any violation of these Rules of the Road.

Source: United Airlines Reservation Center, Sterling, Virginia.

FIGURE 5.2

Summa Health System Mission and Values

Summa exists to serve and to provide compassionate quality care to its patients. Our mission statement reflects this fundamental premise, and our values provide the framework for each of us to support the mission in our day-to-day work.

Patient

OUR MISSION   *The mission of each individual in Summa Health System is to provide quality patient care by supporting the Patient/Nurse/Physician relationship.*

Nurse   Physician

OUR VALUES   Summa strives to create and foster a work environment in which its employees have an opportunity to learn, contribute, and grow. It is an environment that places quality patient care as the core of our work, with constant vigilance to education and research as vital links to that quality care.

Our values reflect tradition. They also define our vision and our quest for quality. They are an affirmation of what is most important for the success of our organization: a *belief* that success is a personal standard . . . compelling us to reach for our highest potential as individuals in service to our community.

- We believe in maintaining the highest standards of personal and organizational integrity. Honesty and fairness are virtues to be commended and embraced.

- We believe in valuing one another. Each employee should value the knowledge, experience, and ability of other employees and the contribution that each makes to Summa.

- We believe in the individuality of our employees. We value diversity in experiences and perspectives at all levels of our work force. Differing points of view should be sought and respected.

- We believe all employees deserve respect and fair treatment. Each employee should support these fundamental premises by being an example of this positive behavior.

- We believe in open communication. Each employee should continually strive to remove communication barriers by getting to know fellow employees. Group participation is encouraged in the resolution of issues.

- We believe in teamwork. We value the participative process and consensus building. It is through cooperation, rather than conflict, that our greatest successes will be derived.

- We believe in preserving a quality, caring organizational environment. Each employee should take responsibility for continuously improving the quality of care and services he or she provides.

- We believe in community service. We exist to meet the health needs of our community. We encourage our employees to be good community citizens and to seek opportunities of service to others.

Member Hospitals: Akron City Hospital/St. Thomas Medical Center

Source: Summa Health System, Akron, Ohio.

All these corporations have identified the qualities they believe are critical to daily work. They make these qualities explicit to employees, managers, customers, and the external world. Each has established a process to collect data regarding performance in relation to these behaviors and skills. Each also expects continuous progress toward improved quality.

The challenge for schools is to guide students and staff to view school as a workplace for all who come together there: students, teachers, administrators, and other personnel. Schools also must teach the skills of a work ethic within the school as a workplace, and they must teach those skills to *all* students. Thus, it's also a challenge to create conditions that give students an opportunity to know expectations, to practice them, and to modify their actions based on feedback from a variety of sources.

CLEAR VISION

To create the conditions where a work ethic can flourish, we first must establish a clear vision of what we want students to know and be able to do. These specific expectations should focus on work ethic, content, and process skills. What would we expect if students were demonstrating a work ethic? Here are some possibilities:

- Students would follow directions.
- Students would complete work.
- Students would be punctual.
- Students would be responsible by setting goals and completing tasks.
- Students would listen with empathy and support to others.
- Students would work effectively as members of a variety of teams.
- Students would demonstrate self-control by decreasing impulsivity and being persistent.

The Community Schools of Ankeny, Iowa, including staff, students, parents, and businesspeople, developed a "Vision for a Graduate from the Ankeny, Iowa, Community Schools." One aspect of the district's essential learnings was defined as "Citizenship and Social Responsibility." This definition included the description of a graduate who

- Determines goals and set priorities.
- Examines options and selects appropriate actions and evaluates progress.

- Demonstrates perseverance.
- Demonstrates respect for self and the diversity of others.
- Functions as a productive member of society.

Carrollton-Farmers Branch Independent School District in Texas adopted a "Vision of a Graduate" that also includes the skills of a work ethic (see Figure 5.3). The Manufacturing and Pre-Engineering Academy in Ohio is committed to preparing students for any level of work. One cornerstone of their initiative is to promote self-directed learning. Figure 5.4 contains a description that is distributed to all staff, students, parents, and business partners involved in the academy. The academy is also working on a process to assess student progress toward these goals in all content areas and to constantly strive for improved performance.

FIGURE 5.3

Graduate Profile

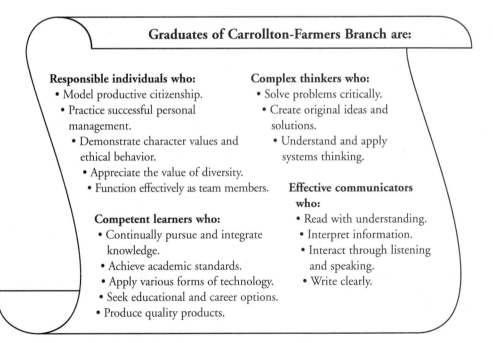

Graduates of Carrollton-Farmers Branch are:

Responsible individuals who:
- Model productive citizenship.
- Practice successful personal management.
- Demonstrate character values and ethical behavior.
- Appreciate the value of diversity.
- Function effectively as team members.

Competent learners who:
- Continually pursue and integrate knowledge.
- Achieve academic standards.
- Apply various forms of technology.
- Seek educational and career options.
- Produce quality products.

Complex thinkers who:
- Solve problems critically.
- Create original ideas and solutions.
- Understand and apply systems thinking.

Effective communicators who:
- Read with understanding.
- Interpret information.
- Interact through listening and speaking.
- Write clearly.

Source: Carrollton-Farmers Branch Independent School District Graduate Profile Task Force, Carrollton, Texas.

FIGURE 5.4

Defining Self-Directed Learning

MANUFACTURING AND PRE-ENGINEERING ACADEMY
1998–99

Self-Directed Learning Is . . .

Initiating and Completing Tasks
- Develops a plan including: a description of the task, strategies, time line, resources.
- Checks work against a set of criteria.
- Makes ongoing modifications based on checking the criteria.
- Raises questions for clarification.
- Generates resources beyond those provided.
- Creates innovative ways to respond to the task.
- Completes the task.
- Articulates the process used in initiating and completing the task.
- Goes beyond the assignment; does more than is required.

Planning and Management
- Attends class and arrives on time.
- Sets goals.
- Plans and follows through with goals, assignments, projects, etc.
- Uses a planning tool such as unit/project plans, weekly plans, daily plans.
- Indicates verbally or in writing the steps needed to complete a task/reach a goal.
- Brings appropriate materials to class.
- Meets deadlines.
- Requests make-up and/or enrichment work and completes it according to the established time line.
- Self-assesses and modifies work based on feedback.

Self-Assessment
- Takes pride in work.
- Recognizes strengths and weaknesses.
- Explains expectations and standards.
- Explains/verbalizes purpose of assessment.
- Uses a variety of assessment techniques (oral, critique, written, symbolic, etc.).
- Seeks feedback from peers and/or teachers, others.
- Within each technique uses a variety of tools (checklists, rubrics, other evaluation scales).
- Monitors and modifies progress according to plans, goals, feedback, etc.
- Communicates and discusses progress with others.
- Explains how end product demonstrates learning.
- Explains strengths and weaknesses of processes used in creating the finished product.

Problem Solving/Decision Making
- Recognizes and states problems.
- States varied perspectives on the problem.
- Investigates why it is a problem.
- Explores/generates multiple solutions/strategies.
- Uses various methods and resources to create possible solutions.
- Evaluates potential solutions.
- Identifies a viable solution and states the rationale.
- Seeks out assistance when alternatives have been exhausted.

Source: Six District Educational Compact, Hudson, Ohio.

BENCHMARKS AND GOALS

After a vision is created, schools have a two-fold task. The first is to define the vision in terms of clear descriptors and indicators. The second is to establish appropriate benchmarks or goals.

Students, staff, and community must understand clearly what the vision means and what it looks like when it becomes a reality. Schools must ensure that everyone shares an understanding of what each statement in the vision means and how it would be demonstrated. For example, teachers in several Ohio districts worked with the habits of mind. They created examples of what a habit might look or sound like if it occurred. They also defined opportunities for gathering evidence or data, and then they created a symbol or logo to characterize the specific habit of mind. Figures 5.5 and 5.6 show examples of their work.

FIGURE 5.5

What Persistence Looks Like

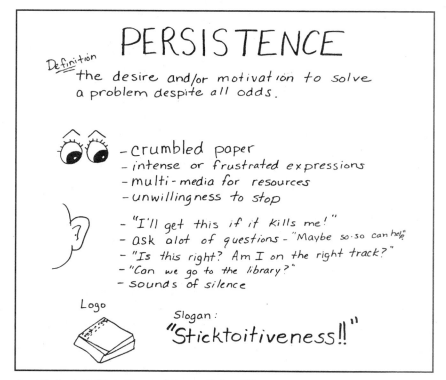

Source: Teachers in Six District Educational Compact, Hudson, Ohio.

FIGURE 5.6

What Checking for Accuracy Looks Like

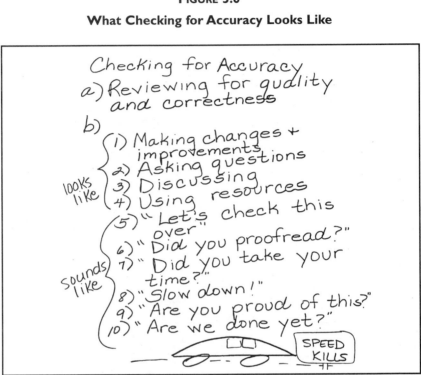

Source: Teachers in Six District Educational Compact, Hudson, Ohio.

These examples helped staff and students clarify the meaning of the habits. They also helped establish a clear picture of what it would look like if a habit occurred. A logo or slogan can also symbolize the desired trait and act as validation when it's put on pins, posters, banners, or t-shirts. This type of reinforcement emphasizes to students, staff, parents, and community members that the habits are important.

Using a different approach, schools should establish a standard for performance in the identified behaviors that will be the goal for all students by the end of 12th grade. This "train schedule" needs to be set with benchmarks at stops along the way that lead to the graduation standard. Figure 5.7 shows how Carrollton-Farmers Branch has created its "Vision of a Graduate" in several areas (Responsible Individuals, Competent Learners, Complex Thinkers, and Effective Communicators). They also have established a series of benchmarks, each delineated by developmentally appropriate competencies and performance behaviors or indicators. (It now remains to create performance tasks that require these behaviors and a process to collect and evaluate the resulting data.)

FIGURE 5.7

Graduate Profile Statement

Responsible Individuals	Grade Level	2	5	8	10	12
Practice successful personal management	*Competency*	Accept responsibility for one's own behavior. Make responsible choices.	Accept responsibility for one's own behavior and wellness. Allocate resources appropriately. Engage in regular physical activity to build lifelong fitness.	Accept responsibility for one's own choices and behavior and wellness. Allocate resources appropriately. Demonstrate organizational skills and strong work ethic.	Accept responsibility for one's own behavior and wellness. Develop effective plans for action. Demonstrate organizational skills and strong work ethic.	Accept responsibility for one's own behavior and wellness. Develop effective plans for action. Demonstrate organizational skills and strong work ethic.
	Sample Performance Behavior	Use class time productively. Manage learning materials and supplies effectively. And others.	Demonstrate organizational skills. Prioritize the use of time and energy. And others.	Set goals, plan, implement, and assess achievement. Recognize needs and utilize resources. Plan and organize projects. And others.	Organize time and resources among study, activities, work, and friends. Be punctual and prepared for classes and activities. Recognize and demonstrate proper behaviors. And others.	Select or develop an organizational system to allocate time and resources. Be punctual and prepared to accept consequences and/or defend actions appropriately. Recognize and demonstrate proper behaviors. And others.

Source: Carrollton-Farmers Branch Independent School District, Division of Instruction and Learning, April 7, 1998.

71

LESSON DESIGN

At this point, the behaviors and skills of the work ethic need to be explicitly included in the lesson design. When a teacher plans a lesson or unit, he considers many factors, identifying some of them as especially important. What content learnings are the focus of the lesson? Are there process areas (thinking, communication, collaboration) that will be required? Specifically, what are they? Are there habits of mind, work ethic behaviors, or other dispositions that will also be required for students to demonstrate their learning?

For example, consider a study of the Constitution. The purpose of the study is for students to understand how individual rights are guaranteed under the Constitution, specifically in the Bill of Rights. It is also critical for them to understand that a set of values is inherent in the Bill of Rights. They will participate in a group task where they study the Bill of Rights, identify the values underscoring the document, and discuss how the document influences their daily lives and the lives of friends and family. The group will then examine documents from other countries and compare and contrast any of their guarantees of individual rights. The grouping structure promotes an analysis where each student in a group of four researches a different country. Students also look at each country's form of government (for example, dictatorship or democracy) to see how the form of government influences the guarantee of individual rights.

The content and skills to be taught in such a lesson must be identified specifically in the design process. A method for tracking what content, process, and habits of mind are presented needs to be developed along with a system for monitoring student performance. For this study of the Constitution, what knowledge and skills might the lesson design involve? Figure 5.8 summarizes how a teacher might detail a lesson's process, content, and habits of mind. This kind of organizer can help a teacher clarify areas of emphasis, gaps that need to be addressed in future lessons, and individual students' progress in meeting the established standards.

MONITORING AND MODIFYING

At this point, identified skills and behaviors need to be taught with established systems for students and teachers to monitor and modify performance. We often teach reading and math skills to students by explicitly identifying the skills or processes, demonstrating the method to be used,

FIGURE 5.8

Organizing a Lesson Design

Knowledge/Content	Process Skills	Habits of Mind
1. Constitution 2. Values/Influences What do we mean by values? What influences values? How are a country's values reflected in its view of individual rights?	1. *Thinking* Analyzes. Compares and contrasts. Indicates a perspective or point of view. 2. *Collaboration* Develops an individual plan and contributes to group plan. Completes tasks of individual plan and contributes to goals of group plan.	1. *Listening with understanding and empathy* Paraphrases. Verbalizes accepting language. 2. *Persisting* Uses a variety of information sources. Seeks feedback from members of the group. Completes task in a timely manner.

and giving practice and feedback about the quality of performance. An expectation that student performance will be timely, responsible, and committed requires the same instructional cycle.

In *Designing Groupwork: Strategies for the Heterogeneous Classroom,* Elizabeth Cohen specifies a process to help students understand and master specific behaviors:

When Teaching New Behaviors . . .
- New behaviors must be labeled and discussed.
- Students must learn to recognize when new behaviors occur.
- Students must be able to use labels and discuss behavior in an objective way.
- Students must have a chance to practice new behaviors.
- New behaviors must be reinforced when they occur (Cohen, 1994, p. 48).

Teachers often need to role-play specific examples of behaviors so students clearly understand what is meant by something like "striving for accuracy." What will a student do that tells others the student is demonstrating the behavior of striving for accuracy? What are the indicators? The teacher might develop a signal such as a thumbs-up to acknowledge when a student demonstrates the behavior. Students should have opportunities to practice demonstrating the behavior and to receive feedback before a more formal assessment task. Many students *could* perform in ways valued by schools, parents, and communities if they understood what the expectations really meant and were given assistance in learning the behaviors.

At Potomac Falls High School in Loudoun County, Virginia, David Holt has developed a unit in a 10th grade English class to explore conflict and interpersonal communications through literature and film. As part of the unit, students read the play *Twelve Angry Men*. They participate on a mock jury where they decide the fate of an accused murderer. The final evaluation is based on the *process* used to arrive at the verdict, which is judged by teacher observation, self-analysis, and peer evaluation. All these analyses contribute to the final evaluation of the project. Figure 5.9 shows the criteria used to assess performance as a juror.

ROLE OF THE TEACHER

Amid all this other work, teachers need to rethink their roles and how they could better influence student performance. For example, the concept of apprenticeship is familiar to most of us. An aspiring physician serves an internship and residency. A lawyer clerks in a law office or with a judge. An aspiring carpenter apprentices with another carpenter, to learn by watching and imitating the senior carpenter's behaviors. In studying the results of student internships or apprenticeships, research found that these experiences are different from typical classrooms as viewed by students (Steinberg, 1997, p. 72). In apprenticeship classrooms,

• Students experience a stronger need to know and find out.
• Students work alongside adults who coach them in the skills necessary to become more productive and valued employees.
• Students begin to understand real-world expectations and what is involved in accomplished performances.

Have you ever considered that students could be considered in an apprenticeship with their teachers? Wouldn't it be wonderful if we could say, "This year you are apprenticing with your teacher in the area of learning/ cognition? By watching and working with your teacher, you will know

FIGURE 5.9

Jury Duty Performance Assessment

Jury Duty Experience Name _____

Use this sheet to perform a self-evaluation and then a group evaluation. The grid on the left is for your self-evaluation, and the grid on the right is for the group evaluation.

Give a score between 1 and 5 for each item.
5=Almost always; 4=A lot; 3=Half of the time; 2=Rarely; 1=Hardly at all.

Carefully consider the entire experience before responding and then answer honestly.

Self-Evaluation		*Group Evaluation*	
Shared opinions and thoughts with the group.		Group identified a leader(s) and/or other roles (e.g., note taker).	
Defended and supported personal point of view with facts.		Group was careful to consider everyone's point of view.	
Listened to and respected others' points of view.		Group made everyone feel welcome and was interested in involving everyone.	
Raised questions that were relevant to the task.		Group was systematic in getting through all the information.	
Added to and built on others' ideas.		Group stayed on task.	
Was willing to change opinion and ideas based on others' contributions.		Group looked at things from various angles and points of view.	
Helped to summarize and paraphrase concepts.		Group stayed calm and rational and avoided chaos and lack of order.	
Allowed others to share and didn't dominate the group.		Group supported one another and found ways to get along with one another.	
Kept on task with related information.		Group felt satisfied with its accomplishments.	
Was polite and respectful when speaking to others in the group.		Group accomplished the task at hand in an organized and timely manner.	

Source: David Holt, Teacher, Grade 10 English, Potomac Falls High School, Loudoun County, Virginia.

what a person does when that person learns and thinks." This model has been presented by Allan Collins and John Seely Brown, and it is discussed by Sylvia Farnham-Diggory (1990) in the book *Schooling: The Developing Child.* Figure 5.10 shows one way to reconceptualize the role of the teacher.

FIGURE 5.10
Role of the Teacher

Modeling: Modeling of what we want students to do. If students need to be excited about their work, teachers need to be excited about their work. If we want students to be thoughtful, we need to demonstrate what thoughtfulness looks like.

Coaching: Helping students to think through what they are trying to do. The teacher raises questions rather than tells students what to do.

Scaffolding and Fading: Providing the content bridges necessary for the task, raising the necessary questions, and giving students the opportunities to explore and perform the task.

Articulation: Explaining what the teacher is thinking about so thinking is visible to the student.

Reflection: Being reflective and thoughtful about the work. Raising evaluation questions. What went well today? Why? If I did this again, how would I do it differently?

Exploration: Modeling risk taking so students understand that uncertainty is involved in all new learning.

If we want students to perform in ways that demonstrate not only content, knowledge, and skills but also a strong work ethic, then *we* need to perform in the same ways. Students in a Virginia high school were discussing student responsibility. They talked about student behaviors that would indicate responsibility. When asked how could teachers help students become more responsible, besides setting clear expectations and providing feedback, they said, "If teachers were more excited about their work, we would feel a greater sense of responsibility. If they don't care, why should we?"

Teachers in the middle schools in Harlandale Independent School District, San Antonio, Texas, met in teaching teams to discuss expectations for students. Each teacher developed a set of expectations for themselves in relation to their team performance, summarized in Figure 5.11. These teachers now are in the process of developing indicators for these expectations and assessment practices to help increase the quality of their team performance.

FIGURE 5.11

Defining "RESPECT"

R — RESPECT. Listen to each other, respect differing opinions.

E — EFFORT. Attend meetings, do your job, participate in decision-making process.

S — SUCCESS. Promote goals and objectives established by team.

P — POSITIVE ATTITUDE. Establish an open-minded environment.

E — EXCELLENCE. Strive for high performance.

C — COORDINATION. Have same goals and objective to maximize achievement.

T — TEAMWORK. Collaborate to affect learning.

Source: Harlandale Independent School District, San Antonio, Texas.

Parents, educators, and the business community consistently agree on these desired behaviors and skills for students. As educators, we can help students develop and perform those skills. Even further, the behaviors and skills are desirable not only for students but for *all* of us. What we want for one student is what we should want for ourselves.

Schools are a workplace for the adults and students who work in them. All of us must constantly strive to improve our performances in those areas identified as critical. At that point, our vision of the work ethic will become a shared vision that benefits everyone.

REFERENCES

Cohen, E. (1994). *Designing groupwork: Strategies for the heterogeneous classroom* (2nd ed.). New York: Teachers College Press.

Farnham-Diggory, S. (1990). *Schooling: The developing child.* Cambridge, MA: Harvard University Press.

Pritchett, P. (1994). *Employee handbook for a radically changing world: 13 ground rules for job success in the information age.* Dallas, TX: Pritchett & Associates.

Steinberg, A. (1997, March/April). A change in the basics: Today's graduates need more than the 3Rs. *The Harvard Education Letter, XIII*(2), 72.

U.S. Department of Labor. (1991, June). *What work requires of schools: A SCANS report for America 2000.* (Report No. 911203). Washington, DC: U.S. Government Printing Office.

THE IMPACT OF
HABITS OF MIND

ARTHUR L. COSTA AND BENA KALLICK

A t this point in your reading, a logical question would be, "If we adopt and implement the habits of mind, how will they affect student learning, teachers and teaching, staff members, school culture, and the community?"

When considering this question, it's important to first realize that the effects of teaching the habits of mind are not immediate. Many experiences, encounters, reflections, rehearsals, practice sessions, and instructions form a habit. Teachers, however, soon do form the habit of teaching the vocabulary of the habits of mind, deliberately structuring questions and inviting students to plan for and reflect on their use of the habits. Students soon begin using that vocabulary. They learn to recognize the performance of the habits of mind in themselves and others, and they discuss ways they could improve that performance. Teachers and students grow beyond the conscious stage as they internalize the habits of mind. The habits become intuitive, ultimately reaching "automaticity." The individual strands (behaviors) eventually are woven into a strong cable (habit).

In working with many schools throughout the United States and internationally, we have collected many examples, indicators, and assessments that demonstrate the impact of adopting, integrating, and infusing the habits of mind into teaching, learning, assessment, and school culture. What follows is a composite of what we have experienced. We've also included testimonials from those who have learned from, lived, and experienced the benefits of the habits of mind.

LEARNING AND LIVING THE HABITS OF MIND

Consider this scene: Faculty members sit scattered around the library. Many arrived early so they could get a coveted seat behind a shelf of books. Though they know they are there for a decisive meeting about a student dress code, they want the seats behind the bookshelves so they can take out papers to grade or newspapers to read. The principal struggles mightily to get their attention about the powerful dress code question. She also struggles with how she can move the faculty from functioning as a group of individuals, each acting on individual beliefs, to a group of individuals acting collectively on a shared set of beliefs.

Does this scene sound familiar? It's a dilemma for many educators that the culture outside of school has become more individualistic, thus affecting culture inside the school. Now more than ever, gaining loyalty to a collective agreement is difficult. As society becomes increasingly more accepting of behavior differences, schools are pressed to accommodate those differences and, at the same time, establish a uniform code of behavior for thinking and learning.

If we were to replay the faculty meeting described earlier with the habits of mind as guiding principles, it might look like this: Staff members enter the room having studied the pros and cons of the decision to be made. The principal starts the meeting by inviting participants to identify the habits of mind that will be used so they all are thoughtful about their decision. The faculty members, familiar with the habits of mind, agree to practice applying past knowledge to new situations, thinking flexibly, and listening with understanding and empathy.

Next, the staff members are given data from the students' perspective, the parents' perspective, and the teachers' and administrators' perspectives. They then break into groups of four. Each group has a process observer. Group members discuss the issue from the various perspectives they've heard, and using a strategy for decision making, they begin to lay out the positive and negative aspects of the decision. After the groups share their recommendations, the whole group discusses the differences and finally reaches consensus.

Now participants return to their small groups. Here the process observer gives them feedback regarding the habits that they agreed to use in their communication with one another. Then, the faculty as a whole reflects on its behavior, and using the observers' feedback, they make explicit some ideas for improving their collaboration in future meetings and interactions.

Does this scenario sound unlikely? Impossible, you say? It may seem so. Although this scenario is a composite, this kind of work is already happening in schools where the habits of mind have been adopted as a shared vision for the entire school community.

SHARED VISION

Loyalty to a process for interaction is as significant as loyalty to the decisions that are a result of that process. We are seeking to operate in a world that is civil, respects individuality and differences, and provides a path for consistency, not uniformity. Because schools are about learning, the habits of mind offer a set of behaviors toward which teachers and students consciously and consistently work. Too often, though, agreeing about a dress code is easier than agreeing about a set of values about the intellect. Perhaps the reason is that agreements about values require changes of behavior in the entire school community, whereas agreements about something like clothing mainly require changes for students.

Senge (1990) suggests that a culture is people thinking together. As individuals share meaning, they negotiate and build a culture. As groups become more skillful in employing the habits of mind, the habits create a renegotiation of the organization by pervading the value system. This change results in the changing of practices and beliefs of the entire organization. By employing the habits of mind, the group mind illuminates issues, solves problems, and accommodates differences. Also through the habits of mind, the group builds an atmosphere of trust in human relationships, trust in the processes of interaction, and trust throughout the organization. The habits of mind facilitate the creation of a shared vision (Senge, 1990).

Suppose a school adopted a vision about the habits of mind that was shared by the entire staff. Grade levels and subject areas would be transcended. The vision would lead to a commitment to a consistent set of behaviors that would build a learning community. These behaviors and dispositions would be more likely to be achieved because they would be reinforced, transferred, and revisited throughout the school, at home, and in the community.

With a focus on habits of mind, educators can overcome the historical isolation, disparity, and episodic nature of teaching and learning. Each class can reinforce the values put forth by the habits of mind. For example, persistence is as valued in social sciences as it is in music, math, and physical education. All teachers, regardless of subject area or grade level, can agree on these desirable qualities. And the community can affirm these qualities, too. Listening with understanding and empathy can be actively pursued by a school board and at a town meeting. The dispositions are just as applicable to developing adult capacities for effective problem solving and continuous learning. All members of the learning organization can continue to become more thoughtful. Then, the outcomes for students and the work culture of the school become congruent and synonymous.

In this type of environment, activities still are taught. Content is selected for its generative nature, and processes are practiced, but they now accumulate into grander, more long-range outcomes. Instructional teams decide: What dispositions do we want students to develop and employ? What will we do to assist their development? How can we work collaboratively to determine if students are developing such dispositions over time? What will we see or hear in student behaviors as evidence of their growth? How might we practice and assess our own growth toward these habits of mind through our work together? Consider these classroom examples:

• Students in a 4th grade class are studying the state of Michigan. They are asked to write a letter to a businessperson to learn how business and industry affects the state economy. At the same time, they are learning about the habits of mind, and they also ask their business contacts whether the habits of mind are practiced in the workplace.

• A high school English teacher asks her students to analyze a novel, using the habits of mind as a lens for interpreting the characters' behaviors. For example, she asks, "Where do you see Huck using habits of mind in this chapter from *Huckleberry Finn*? If he were to use one of the habits as a way to help him out of the problem he faces, which of those habits might be most useful?"

• Students are asked to form cooperative groups. The teacher puts a large chart on the wall before they begin to work on their task (Figure 6.1). She says, "For this task, you will need to persist in your thinking. Let's fill in this chart with what it would look like if your group were persisting on this task. Then we will fill in the chart with what it would sound like if your group were persisting." Notice that this teacher is using the habits of mind as an integral part of the group process. She considers the habits of mind as necessary social behaviors. The group needs to develop a response to the task that is more thoughtful than any single individual might have developed alone.

FIGURE 6.1

What Does Persistence Look Like?

PERSISTENCE	
What would it look like? *What would it sound like?*	
LOOKS LIKE	SOUNDS LIKE
• Staying with the task. • Working through frustration.	• Don't give up. • Let's try this another way.

BUILDING INTEGRITY IN THE SYSTEM

The behaviors of the habits of mind must be practiced regularly. In other words, we must walk the talk. We must also recognize that we already have a habituated set of behaviors, and we will be working to replace one set with another. If the school community's set of habits currently reflects poor communication skills, people unwilling to take responsibility for their own learning, and a lack of respect for multiple perspectives, then beginning to use the habits of mind will constitute a significant replacement of one set of behaviors for another. Anyone who has tried to diet knows the difficulty of changing habits!

The key to change is to

1. Consciously name the new direction. Be explicit about the change.
2. Give the new behaviors meaning through language, visual representations, and examples.
3. Set goals that represent incremental and real conditions that can be met.
4. Establish an assessment and feedback strategy for measuring goals.
5. Celebrate successes.
6. Stay loyal to the change, even when it feels uncomfortable.

As individuals, we organize around identities and beliefs. When we voluntarily join groups, we usually want to be identified with the values that group represents. So it is with an organization. When a shared identity is created through the process of determining purpose, values, and vision, a powerful sense of direction in an otherwise uncertain environment is created. If the organization's purpose, values, and vision are not shared and internalized by all members, "miniorganizations" that do not add up to a system result. Perhaps a department has worked to create its own purpose, values, and vision. That department will self-organize around those beliefs. Perhaps another department has not done this work. The people in that department will organize individually around personal beliefs. With the absence of shared purpose, values, and vision, the self-organization in the group as a whole will be fragmented at various levels, and there will be incongruence in the organization. Pettiness, competition, and self-serving behavior will prevail.

With a focus on the habits of mind as outcomes, the school creates partnerships that transcend traditional boundaries, roles, and grade levels, so stakeholders feel responsible for the whole. Staff, parents, and students become committed to a shared destiny: for the students, themselves, and the organization. As David Bohm (1990) observes,

> The power of a group . . . could be compared to a laser. Ordinary light is called "incoherent," which means that it is going in all sorts of directions, and the light waves are not in phase with each other so they don't build up. But a laser produces a very intense beam that *is* coherent. The light waves build up strength because they are all going in the same direction. This beam can do all sorts of things that ordinary light cannot.

> [O]rdinary thought in society is incoherent—it is going in all sorts of directions with thoughts conflicting and canceling each other out. But if people were to think together in a coherent way, it would have tremendous power. That's the suggestion. If we have a dialogue situation—a group which has sustained dialogue for quite a while in which people get to know each other[—]then we might have such a coherent movement of thought, a coherent movement of communication (pp. 7–8).

Using this analogy to a laser, Figure 6.2 shows arrows going in different directions. With such diffusion, there is no force of directionality. Although each arrow has a trajectory, it often is counter to the direction of another arrow. When you consider living and learning in such an organization, this figure suggests that considerable energy will be placed on "staying out of each other's way." Yet when the arrows are all moving in the same direction, the path has a force. When we work in such a group, we have a sense of where we are going and feel the shoulder-to-shoulder strength of moving toward that place. When our directional force is stated in terms of values regarding thoughtful behaviors, we have better assurance that our ultimate goal of building a learning organization for all members of the school community can be realized.

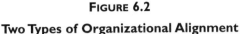

FIGURE 6.2

Two Types of Organizational Alignment

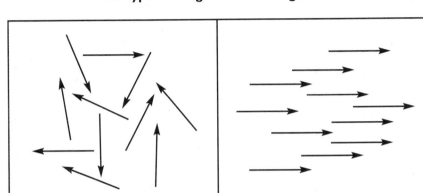

The habits of mind promote common communication behaviors. This promotion is important because people behave similarly in school communities. When we observe an interaction between a secretary and parent, a teacher and student, or a board member and superintendent, we see similarities and can infer from them the basic values of the organization. Margaret Wheatley (1992) describes this phenomenon as the organization having a "fractal" quality. In the best of organizations, one can watch any member to infer the organization's values:

> The very best organizations have a fractal quality to them. An observer of such an organization can tell what the organization's values and ways of doing business are by watching anyone, whether it is a production floor employee or a senior manager. There is consistency and predictability to the quality of behavior. No matter where we look in these organizations, self-similarity is found in its people, in spite of the complex range of roles and levels (p. 32).

Shared identity and beliefs provide direction for an organization without the control that is often characterized as uniformity. Instead, the organization has a pervasive consistency about what is important, which allows for a high degree of individuality to be expressed. The leadership of such organizations must create, articulate, and weave the habits of mind into vision, values, and purposes, the very fiber of the organization, and leaders must be responsible for living them.

IMPLEMENTING THE HABITS

After four years of working with the habits of mind, the staff members of Royal School in Honolulu, Hawaii, were asked to collect indicators of the impact of their efforts and to present their ideas graphically in three areas: impact on teachers' instructional strategies, impact on student learning, and impact on the school culture. They decided to compose before and after charts. Figures 6.3 through 6.5 show these charts and what the students discovered.

At the Colegio Santiago Leon de Caracas in Venezuela, Ingrid Bardasz, a staff member in the Institutional Evaluation Department, described their work with the habits of mind in this way:

> The Institutional Evaluation Department renders services to the whole institution. In performing this complex and demanding task, we relate to many people, and many people are affected by our work. Therefore, we must always have a clear idea about what we do, why we do it, and whom we do it for. Three specific behaviors allow us to reorient the way we conduct our work: listening to others with understanding and empathy, checking for accuracy and precision, and drawing on past knowledge.
>
> At the beginning of the school year we carried out an exercise to check every member's expectations. At that moment, some intelligent behaviors began to pop up: listening to others with understanding and empathy, and checking for accuracy. It was amazing to find that two members decided to work on flexibility and managing impulsivity on a personal basis, as both of these habits of mind have influenced their own behavior, as well as their relationships with others. Just verbalizing it was crucial. However, the process has gone beyond a mere statement, and now we hold weekly work-meetings, where feelings can be shared and everyone listens empathically. This has been wonderful because it enriches the group in a natural way.
>
> We strive for accuracy and precision by checking one another's outputs, and everyone gives their opinion about how to improve them. As a

FIGURE 6.3

Impact on Instruction

Before the habits of mind, a visitor would

SEE	HEAR
Teacher lecturing. Teacher accepting only one answer.	Teacher-dominated talk.
Student passivity.	Quiet.
Students unaware of grading criteria.	Teacher judgments.
Grades and report cards.	
	Teacher lecturing/telling/giving information.
Test-oriented worksheets and drills.	Literal questioning.

After the habits of mind, a visitor would

SEE	HEAR
Student-to-student interaction.	Socratic dialogue.
Student participation and questioning.	Busy noise.
Open-ended evaluation.	Student self-evaluation. Rubrics, checklists, and portfolios.
Students listening.	
Project-based learning.	
Use of graphic organizers.	Collaborative hum.

FIGURE 6.4

Impact on Student Learning

Before the habits of mind, a visitor would	
SEE	**HEAR**
Students seated at individual desks.	
	No awareness of habits of mind.
	Students reluctant to give original opinions.
	Students offering one idea.
	Students giving short answers.
Hands-off activities.	
Passive students.	

After the habits of mind, a visitor would	
SEE	**HEAR**
Cooperative groups.	
	Students using the habits of mind vocabulary.
	Students eager to share ideas.
	Many students offering several ideas.
	Elaborated answers with supporting data or rationale.
Hands-on activities.	
Eager students.	

FIGURE 6.5

Impact on School Culture and Environment

Before the habits of mind, a visitor would	
SEE	**HEAR**
Bare walls.	
Teachers working in isolation.	
	Quiet classrooms.
No mention of habits of mind in newsletters.	
	No awareness of habits of mind.
Absence of criteria for performance.	
Student sent to office or counselor for disciplining.	
Mediocre test score results.	

After the habits of mind, a visitor would	
SEE	**HEAR**
Habits of mind posted in classrooms and corridors.	
Teachers collaborating.	
	Humor and laughter.
Newsletters sent home to parents celebrating performances of habits of mind.	
Public recognition of performance of habits of mind.	
Public, explicit criteria for performance.	
Reduction in office referrals.	
Higher scores on standardized tests.	

result, these tasks have been carried out fluidly, errors have been reduced, and delivery times have been improved. We also use checking at a communicational level when someone feels uncomfortable about something.

We have been practicing thinking flexibly. We allow ourselves to stop a discussion when it's needed without feeling that we are not on task, not fulfilling our obligations, or are losing time. We bend to situations or decisions where taking a rigid stance would only hinder our work. We understand others' needs and, based on that understanding, we employ a consulting process, which is this department's main role. We feel good practicing communication and listening attentively and with understanding. We understand the value of drawing from previous experiences. We always had referenced them by asking, how was this done before? However, now we do it consciously to see if something should be changed.

We decided to practice little by little. We began with those behaviors needing improvement in the short term because they were affecting our productivity. We are very grateful for this contribution to our personal and professional growth. We think that making a practice of the habits of mind, in addition to making us better individuals, will make us achieve better intra and inter-department performance.

No one ever "achieves mastery" of the habits of mind. Yet all of us can continue to perfect our performance, to develop our capacities, to be more alert to opportunities for their use, and to employ the habits of mind more deliberately throughout our lifetime. What makes the habits of mind "value added" is that they are as suitable for the adults in the school and community as they are for students. All of us practice the habit of remaining open to continuous learning.

REFERENCES

Bohm, D. (1990). *On dialogue.* Ojai, CA: David Bohm Seminars.

Senge, P. (1990). *The fifth discipline: The art and practice of the learning organization.* New York: Doubleday/Currency.

Wheatley, M. (1992). *Leadership and the new science: Learning about organization from an orderly universe.* San Francisco: Berett-Koehler Publishers.

RECOMMENDATIONS FOR
GETTING STARTED

ARTHUR L. COSTA AND BENA KALLICK

We hope that this book has inspired you to introduce the habits of mind to your school community. The most difficult part of such change, however, can be deciding how to get started. This chapter offers practical suggestions from practitioners who already have gone through that process. The ideas they share illustrate meaningful ways any school or district can begin to nurture the habits of mind among students and staff.

LITERATURE CIRCLES

Penn Valley School in Lower Merion, Pennsylvania, created literature circles to study a book that included information about the habits of mind. You might consider forming your own literature circles to study this book (or all of the books in Habits of Mind: A Developmental Series).

Literature circles are small, temporary discussion groups whose members have chosen to read the same story, poem, article, or book. The group determines which portion of the text will be read either inside or outside the meeting. As they read, members prepare to fulfill specific responsibilities in the upcoming discussion. Each comes to the group with the notes needed to help perform that specific job.

The circles have regular meetings, with discussion roles rotating each session. When they finish a book, circle members plan a way to share highlights of their reading with the wider community. Then they trade members among groups, select more reading, and move into a new cycle. Once readers are comfortable with successfully conducting their own wide-ranging, self-sustaining discussions, formal discussion roles may be dropped.

Based on Daniels (1994) and Routman (1991), we have identified these key features of literature circles:

1. Participants choose their own materials.

2. Small, temporary groups are formed on the basis of book or chapter choice.

3. Different groups read different books (or chapters).

4. Groups meet on a regular schedule to discuss their reading.

5. Participants use written or drawn notes to guide both their reading and their discussion.

6. Participants generate discussion topics.

7. Group meetings aim to foster open, natural conversations. Though group members may play specific roles in a discussion, personal connections, digressions, and open-ended questions are welcome.

8. In newly forming groups, participants play a rotating assortment of task roles.

9. The leader serves as a facilitator, not as a group member or instructor.

10. There is self-evaluation.

11. A spirit of playfulness and fun pervades the room.

12. When members complete a book, they share with one another (and with the community). Then new groups form around new reading choices.

Also based on Daniels (1994) and Routman (1991), we have identified a few group roles. You may want to create other roles to satisfy your group's needs. The roles we have described include

- *Discussion Director:* creates a list of questions for the group.
- *Passage Picker:* chooses parts of the book to be read aloud.
- *Connector:* finds connections between the book and the classroom as well as the book and the school community.

Whatever form your group takes, literature circles are a powerful way to explore information in a relaxed but dynamic setting. They provide opportunities to practice communicating with clarity and precision, listening with understanding and empathy, and thinking flexibly by examining alternative points of view. They also offer an experience in continuous learning.

THE POWER OF VISION

All the educational leaders who have helped their districts move to a full-system use of the habits of mind began in the same place: They realized that thinking skills must be an explicit part of a school vision. Though your school or district may not be ready yet to commit to a full-system use of the habits (or maybe you're simply considering using the habits in your own classroom), it's still helpful to envision how the habits of mind will look when they are used.

When you consider the ideas presented in this book, think about how the day would look if only one or two classrooms used the habits of mind. What if the whole school used habits of mind? How would it look if students moved from class to class—and subject to subject—encountering the application of the habits of mind? And what if the whole school community were involved, including parents, board members, and faculty? What would be the implications for school change?

The staff of the Academia Cotopaxi in Quito, Ecuador, began its work with the habits of mind by reading various articles and books in areas such as intelligences, Dimensions of Learning (Marzano, 1992), and Smart Schools (Perkins, 1992). After a two-day workshop on the habits of mind, they decided to create a vision statement to guide their work. Something similar might serve your district or school. They generated their vision statement by posing such questions as

1. What would our curriculum look like if it were infused with the habits of mind?

2. What would assessment look like if we gathered evidence of growth in the habits of mind?

3. What would instruction look like and sound like if we taught toward the habits of mind?

4. How would content be selected if we used it as a vehicle to teach the habits of mind?

5. What would our hiring practices be like if we added staff with the intent of cultivating the habits of mind?

6. What would our school environment look like if it were infused with the habits of mind?

7. What would our daily schedule be like if we adopted the habits of mind?

8. What would teacher-to-teacher interaction sound like if we internalized the habits of mind?

9. What would student-to-student interaction sound like and look like if they habituated the habits of mind?

10. How would we expend our limited resources of money, time, and energy if we valued the habits of mind?

11. What would our reward system be like if it recognized excellence in the habits of mind?

START WITH YOUR OWN STUDENTS

Perhaps you feel you're ready to begin using the habits of mind with your own students. As you observe them working in groups, solving problems, and interacting with others, which habits of mind do you think they need most? You might ask yourself, "What is it about my students that makes me think they need to learn how to think? What do I see them doing, hear them saying, or notice them feeling that indicates they need to learn these habits of mind?"

We do not suggest you start with all 16 of the habits described in this book. Prioritize the list. Share the list with your class and discuss what certain habits of mind would look or sound like if students used them. Are your students impulsive, acting without thinking and blurting out answers? You may wish to start with managing impulsivity. Do your students interrupt each other, laugh at others, or put them down? You may wish to start with the habit of listening with understanding and empathy. Do your students lack awareness of their own problem-solving strategies and their effects on others? You may wish to begin with thinking about thinking (metacognition).

Lisa Davis, a teacher at West Orchard School in Chappaqua, New York, begins to develop the habits of mind right from the start of the school year:

> I start to use the habits of mind in conversation with the kids in September. I begin the year by immersing the children in cooperative activities that require them to problem solve from the moment they walk in the door. For example, the following problem is written on the board on the first day of school: "You may sit at any table provided you meet the following criteria: There is only one person that was in your class last year and your table must be mixed by gender." This problem gives everyone something to do when they come in, which relieves some of the first-day jitters.
>
> When the children finish solving a problem, we discuss what happened. One of the most important things for children to do in school is reflect, especially after cooperative tasks and long-term projects. In order to truly understand a concept, the student needs time to question,

explore, refine his or her thinking, observe, and reflect. Unfortunately, this "think time" tends to be the first thing to go when time is short.

In the beginning of the year, I start the reflective discussions by telling the children what I observed as I was "kidwatching." (As the year progresses the children lead the discussion.) After the problem described above, for example, I noted that Dillon and Matt were very *persistent* because they wanted to sit together, as did Jessa and Lauren. This table of four students met the mixed-gender criterion, but something still wasn't working.

I asked, "Can you tell us what happened?"

Dillon explained, "Matt, Lauren, and I were all in the same class last year, but the only other people that we could trade with also had people that had been in the same class."

Matt clarified, "The problem is that 11 out of 23 of us had Mr. Hill last year. So that means every table will have to have two kids from Mr. Hill's class and one table will have to have three from his class." I asked how they resolved the issue.

Jessa said, "The boys suggested that we do Rock, Paper, Scissors. But then Lauren said she would be willing to sit at this [the neighboring] table as long as I could sit directly across the aisle from her."

Lauren said, "I would have done Rock, Paper, Scissors, but that would have only solved our problem. It wouldn't have solved the whole class problem of putting two kids from Mr. Hill's class at each table."

I thanked the four of them for sharing what went well and what was difficult for them. I emphasized that thinking about everyone in the community was especially impressive. Then I specifically thanked Jessa and Lauren for *taking that risk* on the first day of school. I emphasized that I know how important it is to be near someone you're comfortable with. This short exercise required problem solving and cooperation. It was also an opportunity for me to start identifying behaviors that I would be looking for in the future.

Several school districts have chosen to focus on one of the habits of mind each month. For example, one school staff agreed that students were careless, lacked craftsmanship, and cared little about refinement and checking. They decided to begin working with striving for accuracy. In grade-level meetings at the elementary school and in department meetings at the secondary school, staff members discussed how they could use their subject matter as vehicles for encouraging this particular habit of mind.

Teachers in the various subject areas—industrial arts, music, science, math, and language—agreed they would find opportunities to emphasize the need for accuracy in their subject matter. They ensured that students understood that striving for accuracy was a prerequisite for success in each class.

For example, an industrial arts teacher volunteered, "I give the students one piece of wood and remind them that they had better measure three times before they cut once." The language arts teachers agreed that having students keep portfolios of their work would be another strategy for looking at accuracy. These portfolios would include not only the finished product but also rough drafts and first renditions showing how their writing was perfected with each rewrite. The music teachers eloquently stated that perfection of performance was their ultimate goal. Achieving perfect harmony through practice and even more practice was the musicians' ultimate endeavor.

The beneficiaries of this planning are, of course, the students. As students travel from grade level to grade level throughout the elementary years, or class to class throughout the secondary day, they soon realize that they are encountering the same habits of mind wherever they go. Soon it begins to sink in. They see that the habits of mind transcend all subjects and all classrooms; the habits pervade everything done in the school. Over time, the behaviors become so habituated that students apply them to their daily life. In the following excerpt from a letter from Hectalina Donado, Elementary Principal of Colegio Karl C. Parrish in Baranquilla, Colombia, she explains how her school created this kind of environment:

> At the beginning of the school year, we placed a banner at the entrance to the school featuring our logo, and we began talking to the children about habits of mind [see Figure 7.1]. I conducted two workshops for new teachers and aides to introduce them to the concept and to share the information given to us. A small poster with the same logo was printed and given to teachers in the elementary school to post in a visible place in their classrooms. This same poster was placed all around the school. During our open house, the idea was presented to the parents. Our group of parent volunteers requested that I conduct a workshop for them.
>
> "KCP" pencils are given out to the kids on Fridays during our morning assemblies when we celebrate their birthdays. At this time I remind them about the [habit of mind] being featured. Although the teachers stress all the behaviors within the context of their daily work, we feature one behavior every month. Every month, I ask the children to write about the [habit of mind] being featured and we pick the best composition for display on a special bulletin board [see Figure 7.2 for one student's work].

FIGURE 7.1

Banner from Colegio Karl C. Parrish

KNOWLEDGE
CURIOSITY
PERSEVERANCE

FIGURE 7.2

Orlando's Reflections

Controlling Impulsivity

Controlling impulsivity means to think what I am going to do! One way that I can control my impulsivity is like if I want to run in the class I am going to think that I will run in recess. And another way is that I will not yell the answer because I will disturb my friends. And another way is that I will behave my self. And to control my self. And be a good listener.

ACTIVATING HABITS OF MIND

Another way to begin work with the habits of mind is to complete a chart like the one shown in Figure 7.3. At one school, a group spent several faculty meetings discussing each habit of mind. Then they broke into small groups to complete the cells in the chart. Their task had four components:

1. Describe the habit of mind in their own words.
2. Provide indicators of what they would hear people saying if they were displaying that habit of mind.
3. Provide indicators of what they would see people doing if they were displaying that habit of mind.
4. Describe what it would feel like within the person or what feelings would be produced in the group if that habit of mind were employed.

The charts were posted in the faculty room as a reminder, and additions or refinements were made to each cell over time.

CONCLUSION

This first volume of Habits of Mind: A Developmental Series is an invitation to expand the focus of your educational outcomes to include those broad, enduring, and essential life-span learnings. This book has described some of the dispositions of human beings that are essential to function successfully as effective workers, critical decision makers, loving family members and participatory citizens in a democratic society, and concerned inhabitants of a shrinking world community.

Book 2 of this series, *Activating and Engaging Habits of Mind*, will provide many practical techniques, sample lessons, and instructional strategies from experienced practitioners for cultivating the habits of mind in classrooms, schools, homes, and communities. We are not suggesting that students' need for knowledge be diminished but, rather, that learning activities and content commonly taught in schools be viewed as opportunities to employ, reflect on, and evaluate the use of the habits of mind. As school staffs, parents, and the community work together to recognize, support, and model the habits of mind, students will repeatedly encounter these intelligent behaviors throughout their environment, and thus, over time, these intelligent behaviors will become habituated—they will become habits of mind.

FIGURE 7.3

Describing the Habits of Mind

Habit of Mind	What Is It?	Sounds Like	Looks Like	Feels Like
1. Persisting	Sticking to a task even though you want to give up.	"Hang in there." "Keep at it."	Attending even with distractions. Trying again.	Even though I'd like to quit, I know I have the strength to continue.
2. Managing impulsivity	Thinking before acting.	"Just a minute, let me think."	Looking both ways before crossing the street. Examining directions before beginning a task.	Slow down. Take a deep breath. Count to 10. Pause.
3. Listening with understanding and empathy	Paraphrasing. Attending. Sensing others' feelings.	"So you're suggesting . . ." "Your idea is . . ." "You're upset because . . ."	Facing one another. Eye contact. Nodding.	Comforting. Trusting. Vulnerable.
4. Thinking flexibly	Ability to change your mind. Approaching a problem from a different perspective.	"I think I see things differently now."	Trying different approaches.	Stretching. Hard to give up your own viewpoint but expanding.
5. Thinking about thinking (metacognition)	Thinking about your own thinking.	"Right now, I'm wondering . . ." "My strategy is . . ."		
6. Striving for accuracy	Working toward perfection, elegance, craftsmanship.	"Making a list, checking it twice."	Taking aim.	
7. Questioning and posing problems				
8. Applying past knowledge to new situations		"This reminds me of . . ."		
9. Thinking and communicating with clarity and precision				
10. Gathering data through all senses		"Let me feel it." "Let me taste it." "Let me smell it."		
11. Creating, imagining, innovating				
12. Responding with wonderment and awe		"Wow!" "Cool!" "Aha!"		Fascination. Intrigue. Surprise. Exhilaration.
13. Taking responsible risks		"Let's try it."		
14. Finding humor				
15. Thinking interdependently		"Who else can we involve?"		
16. Remaining open to continuous learning				

REFERENCES

Daniels, H. (1994). *Literature circles: Voice and choice in the student-centered classroom.* York, ME: Stenhouse Publishers.

Marzano, R. J. (1992). *A different kind of classroom: Teaching with Dimensions of Learning.* Alexandria, VA: Association for Supervision and Curriculum Development.

Perkins, D. (1992). *Smart schools: From training memories to educating minds.* New York: The Free Press.

Routman, R. (1991). *Invitations: Changing as teachers and learners K–12.* Portsmouth, NH: Heinemann.

ACKNOWLEDGMENTS

We wish to express our appreciation to the many contributors to this series of books. The descriptions of their experiences, lessons, implementation strategies, vignettes, and artwork are what give meaning, expression, and practicality to the habits of mind. To them we are eternally grateful.

We wish to thank John O'Neil, Nancy Modrak, Julie Houtz, Margaret Oosterman, and other members of the ASCD editorial staff who encouraged and guided us throughout this project. Our gratitude is expressed to our editor, René Bahrenfuss, for her flexibility, her striving for accuracy, and her persistence. We are appreciative of the artistic talents of Georgia McDonald and other ASCD design staff for the habits of mind icons. Without their attention to detail, striving for perfection, and creative imagination, this series could not have come to fruition.

We also wish to thank our assistants, Kim Welborn and Carol Hunsiker, whose secretarial skills and computer wizardry behind the scenes kept us organized and in communication with each other and with all the authors.

We pay particular tribute to Bena's husband, Charles, and Art's wife, Nancy, who tolerated our time away from them. Their love, encouragement, and understanding provided the support base for our success.

Finally, we wish to acknowledge the many teachers, administrators, and parents in the numerous schools and communities throughout the United States and abroad who have adopted and implemented the habits of mind and have found them a meaningful way to organize learning. The future world will be a more thoughtful, compassionate, and cooperative place because of their dedication to cultivating the habits of mind in students and modeling them in their own behavior.

INDEX

Note: An *f* after a page number indicates a reference to a figure. An entry in bold-face refers to one of the 16 habits of mind.

ABOUT THE AUTHORS

Arthur L. Costa is an emeritus professor of education at California State University, Sacramento, and codirector of the Institute for Intelligent Behavior in Cameron Park, California. He has been a classroom teacher, a curriculum consultant, and an assistant superintendent for instruction, as well as the director of educational programs for the National Aeronautics and Space Administration. He has made presentations and conducted workshops in all 50 states, as well as in Mexico, Central and South America, Canada, Australia, New Zealand, Africa, Europe, Asia, and the Islands of the South Pacific.

Costa has written numerous articles and books, including *Techniques for Teaching Thinking* (with Larry Lowery), *The School as a Home for the Mind*, and *Cognitive Coaching: A Foundation for Renaissance Schools* (with Robert Garmston). He is editor of *Developing Minds: A Resource Book for Teaching Thinking* and coeditor (with Rosemarie Liebmann) of the Process as Content Trilogy: *Envisioning Process as Content, Supporting the Spirit of Learning*, and *The Process-Centered School*.

Active in many professional organizations, Costa served as president of the California Association for Supervision and Curriculum Development and as national president of the Association for Supervision and Curriculum Development, 1988–89.

Costa can be reached at Search Models Unlimited, P.O. Box 362, Davis, CA 95617-0362; phone/fax: 530-756-7872; e-mail: artcosta @aol.com.

Bena Kallick is a private consultant providing services to school districts, state departments of education, professional organizations, and public agencies throughout the United States. Kallick received her doctorate in educational evaluation at Union Graduate School. Her areas of focus include group dynamics, creative and critical thinking, and alternative assessment strategies in the classroom. Her written work includes *Literature to Think About* (a whole language curriculum published with Weston Woods Studios), *Changing Schools into Communities for Thinking*, and *Assessment in the Learning Organization* (coauthored with Arthur Costa).

Formerly a Teachers' Center director, Kallick also created a children's museum based on problem solving and invention. She was the coordinator of a high school alternative designed for at-risk students. She is cofounder of TECHPATHS, a company designed to facilitate teachers' networks and communication about performance assessment. Kallick's teaching appointments have included Yale University School of Organization and Management, University of Massachusetts Center for Creative and Critical Thinking, and Union Graduate School. She is on the boards of JOBS for the Future and the Apple Foundation.

Kallick can be reached at 12 Crooked Mile Rd., Westport, CT 06880; phone/fax: 203-227-7261; e-mail: bkallick@aol.com.

Marian Leibowitz is an educational consultant to school districts, state departments of education, professional organizations, and agencies throughout the United States and internationally. Her major areas of focus are in the restructuring of schools: leadership, change, instructional design, curriculum, and assessment.

Leibowitz has been a teacher of the gifted and has served as a consultant to numerous school districts for establishing and evaluating programs serving students with special needs. She is the developer of several audiovisual products, including the ASCD Professional Inquiry Kit *Promoting Learning Through the Use of Student Data.* She is a contributing author to the book *Instruction for Process Learning: Supporting the Spirit of Learning.*

Leibowitz has served as president of the New Jersey Association of Learning Consultants and chapter president for the Council of Exceptional Children. She is past president of the New Jersey Association for Supervision and Curriculum Development.

David Perkins, codirector of Harvard Project Zero, is a senior research associate at the Harvard Graduate School of Education. He is the author of several books, including *Smart Schools: From Training Memories to Educating Minds, Outsmarting IQ: The New Science of Learnable Intelligence,* and *Knowledge as Design,* and many articles. He has helped to develop instructional programs and approaches for teaching understanding and thinking, including initiatives in South Africa, Israel, and Latin America. He is a former Guggenheim Fellow.

Shari Tishman is a research associate at Harvard Project Zero, Harvard Graduate School of Education. Her interests include the development of high-level cognition in the arts and in other areas. She has written extensively about the teaching of thinking, and she has developed a variety of thinking-centered educational materials. Much of her work focuses on the dispositional side of high-level thinking. Among other projects, she has worked with art museums in Massachusetts and New York to develop and assess programs that teach thinking through looking at art.